AF345802

SKETCH OF THE HISTORY OF THE KNIGHTS TEMPLARS

ILLUSTRATED

JAMES BURNES

CONTENTS

TO
HIS ROYAL HIGHNESS
Prince Augustus Frederick.
DUKE OF SUSSEX, EARL OF INVERNESS, K.G.
D.C.L.
&c. &c. &c. &c.
Grand Prior of England,
THE FOLLOWING PAGES ARE DEDICATED
With every sentiment of Respect,
BY
His faithful and obedient Servant and Brother,
JAMES BURNES.

INTRODUCTION.

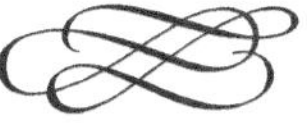

Having learned from some of those kind and esteemed Friends who lately presented to me a magnificent piece of Plate, in the name of the Free Masons of Scotland, on the occasion of my approaching departure for India, that I could not more suitably evince my sense of gratitude, than by leaving amongst them, as a token of remembrance, some Memoir of the Order of the Temple, with which they seem to consider me in some measure identified, I have, in compliance with their wish, devoted the very few hours of leisure I have had during the last month, to the preparation of the following Sketch;— and feel confident, that from an individual almost constantly engaged in arrangements for quitting his Native Country, and labouring under the most painful feelings, at the prospect of parting from his family, and those with whom he has lived in cordial terms of friendship during the last three years, nothing very finished or original will be expected; and I offer no apology, therefore, when I state, that a considerable portion of the following pages consists merely of an abridgement or reprint of an admirable, but not sufficiently known article, written by Mr. Keightly, on the History of the Templars, down to the period of the Persecution, in the Foreign Quarterly Review for 1828, followed by some Extracts from Laurie's Free-Masonry, and Mill's History of Chivalry.

The account of the present state of the Order has been taken from the official "Manuel des Chevaliers de l'Ordre du Temple," published both at Paris and Liverpool; as well as from information gathered either in foreign books, such as the "Acta Latamorum," in which all the Statutes, &c. were given to the Public in 1815, or from conversations with which I have been honoured by His Royal Highness the Duke of Sussex, Admiral Sir William Sidney Smith, General Wright, and other distinguished Templars, at home and abroad. For much of the information recorded in the Chapter on the Scottish Templars, I am under great obligations to Adam Paterson, and William Pringle, Esquires, both of whom furnished me with valuable Manuscripts. The latter of these gentlemen is the author of various papers on the Templars, in that valuable periodical, the Free-Masons' Review, nor was it until I had failed to induce him to give, in a continuous form, the result of his own researches on the subject, that I myself ventured to enter upon the present Work.

In conclusion, I have to express my warmest acknowledgments to my friend, W. A. Laurie, Esquire, Secretary to the Grand Lodge of Scotland, for many valuable notes and additions,—to whose taste and exertions this little Volume owes its appearance before the Public, and to whom personally I am indebted for many favours, which he would not wish me to particularise.

UNITED SERVICE CLUB,
Edinburgh, 28th May 1837.

CHAP. I. THE HOSPITALLERS.

The natural desire to visit places which have been the scene of memorable actions, or the abode of distinguished personages, had from a very early period drawn pious pilgrims from the east and the west to view those spots which had been hallowed by the presence of the Son of God. The toils and the dangers of the journey were unheeded, when set in comparison with the bliss of pouring forth prayer on Calvary, and bathing in the waves of Jordan, whose waters had consecrated the Saviour to his holy office.

And, accordingly, we find that, so early as the ninth century, there was in the valley of Jehoshaphat, near the church of the Holy Virgin, an Hospital composed of twelve dwellings, for pilgrims from the west, which possessed corn lands, vineyards, and gardens, and an excellent library, established by the bounty of Charlemagne.

In the eleventh century, when the apprehension of the approaching end of the world, and appearance of Christ to judge mankind, had once more fanned the flame of pious pilgrimage which had been previously dying away, and men were hastening to the land where they expected to meet their Lord and Judge, there was built within the walls of Jerusalem an Hospital for the reception of Catholic pilgrims. This hospital stood within a very short distance of the church of the Holy Sepulchre, and, by the favour of the Egyptian Khalif, a church, dedicated to the Virgin, and afterwards called St. Maria de Latina, was erected close by it; there an abbot and several monks, who followed the rule of St. Benedict, received and entertained the pilgrims who arrived each year from the west, and furnished such of them as were poor or had been plundered by the roving Bedouins, with the means of paying the tax exacted by the unbelievers. Decorum not permitting the reception of female pilgrims, the brethren established without their walls a convent, dedicated to Mary Magdalene, where a pious sisterhood entertained the pilgrims of their own sex. The number of the pilgrims still continuing to increase, the abbot and his monks erected a new *Hospitium* near their church, which they placed under the patronage of St. John, the Patriarch of Alexandria, named Eleemon, or the Compassionate. This last Hospital had no independent revenues, but derived its income from the bounty of the abbot of the monastery of the Holy Virgin, and the alms of the pious.[1]

When, in 1099, Jerusalem was invested by the Crusaders, the Hospital of St. John was presided over by Gerhard, a native of Provence, a man of exemplary piety, and of a spirit of mild and universal benevolence, rarely to be found in that age; for while the city was pressed by the arms of the faithful, who sought for future glory by the extermination of those whom they deemed the enemies of God on earth, not merely the orthodox Catholic, but the schismatic Greek, and even the unbelieving Moslem, shared without distinction the alms of the good director of the Hospital of St. John. When the city was taken, the sick and wounded of the Crusaders received all due care and attention from Gerhard and his monks. The general favour they enjoyed with Godfrey de Bouillon and the other pilgrims now emboldened them to separate themselves from the monastery of St. Mary de Latina; and to pursue their labour of love alone and independent, they drew up a rule for themselves, to which they bound themselves to obedience in the presence of the patriarch, and assumed as their distinguishing dress, a black mantle, with a white cross of eight points on the left breast.[2] They still remained obedient to the abbot of St. Maria de Latina, and according to the law of the church, they paid tythes to the patriarch.

This continued while the brotherhood was poor; but riches soon began to flow in upon them. Godfrey, whose very name suggests the ideas of virtue and piety, pure, if not always well-directed, struck with their simple and unassuming charity, bestowed on them his domain of Monboire, in Brabant, with all its appurtenances. His brother and successor, Baldwin, gave them a portion of the booty gained from the infidels; several pious princes and nobles followed these examples, and the Hospital of St. John soon saw itself in possession of extensive estates, both in Europe[3] and Asia, which were managed by members of the society named Preceptors. Pope Pascall II, in 1113, relieved the Hospitallers from the burden of paying tythes to the patriarch of Jerusalem—confirmed by his Bull all donations made and to be made to them— and gave them authority to appoint a successor on the death of Gerhard, without the interference of any other secular or spiritual authority. The society now counted among its members many gallant knights who had come to the Holy Land to fight in the cause of their Saviour; and there, actuated by a spirit more accordant to his, had flung aside their swords, and devoted themselves to the attendance on the sick and poor among the brethren of St. John. One of the most distinguished of these was Raymond Dupuy, a knight of Dauphiné, who, on the death of the worthy Gerhard, was chosen to succeed him in his office.

It was Raymond who organized the order of the Hospitallers, and established the discipline of the order. His regulations afford a specimen of the manners and modes of thinking of his time; and some of them require to be noticed here, on account of their similarity with those of the Templars, shortly to be mentioned. The usual monkish duties of chastity and obedience were strictly enjoined; the brethren, both lay and spiritual, were directed to wear at least a linen or woollen shirt, but no expensive dress of any kind; above all, no furs; when they went to collect alms, they were, for fear of temptation, never to go alone, but always in parties of two or three; they were not, however, to select their companions, but to take such as the director should appoint them; wherever there was a house belonging to their order, they were to turn in thither, and nowhere else, and to take whatever was given them, and ask for nothing more; they were also to carry their lights with them, and wherever they passed the night, to set these burning before them, lest the enemy should bring on them some deadly danger. When the brethren were in the church, or in a private house, in the company of women, they were to take good heed to themselves and avoid temptation; for the same reason, they were never to suffer women to wash their head or feet, or to make their bed. If a brother had fallen into carnal sin, and his offence was secret, a silent penance was deemed sufficient; but if it had been public, and he was fully convicted of it, he was on Sunday, after mass, when the people were gone out of church, to be stript of his clothes, and there, by the director himself, or such of the brethren as he appointed, severely beaten with thongs or rods, and then expelled the order. Any brother possessed of money or valuables, who concealed them from the master, was severely punished, the money which he had secreted was hung about the offender's neck, and he was scourged by one of the brethren, in the presence of all those belonging to the house; he had then to do penance for forty days, during which time, on Wednesdays and Fridays, he had nothing but bread and water to support him. These regulations were made by Raymond, in the year 1118; a circumstance to be attended to, as some similar rules have been since made a ground of accusation against the Templars.

It is uncertain whether Raymond had any ulterior design of making the order of the Hospitallers a military one, but if such was his intention, he was anticipated. The kingdom of Jerusalem, over which Baldwin II. now ruled, had been in a very extraordinary state from the date of its conquest. It lay between two enemies, the Egyptians on the south, and the Turks on the north; and these Moslems, though of opposite and hostile sects, agreed in hatred of the Christians, and a desire to take Jerusalem— which was to them also the Holy City—out of the hands of the western infidels; the independent Arabs of the desert were also inimical to the Christians, and as fond of plunder as they have been at all periods of their history. Hence, the Holy Land was continually infested by predatory bands, who robbed and plundered all who fell in their way; the pious pilgrim who disembarked at Joppa or Acre, was fortunate if he reached the ultimate object of his journey in safety; and when he had visited all the consecrated places within the sacred walls, new perils awaited him on his way to bathe in the purifying waters of the Jordan, or to pluck in the gardens of Jericho the palm branch which he was to suspend in the church on his return.

1. "The Greek Convent adjoins the Church of the Holy Sepulchre. From the terrace of this Convent, you see a spacious enclosure, in which grow two or three olive trees, a palm tree, and a few cypresses. The house of the Knights of St. John of Jerusalem formerly occupied this deserted spot."—Chateaubriand.

2. At a subsequent period, the war-dress of the Knights Hospitallers was a scarlet tunic, or sopra vest, on which was embroidered the sacred emblem of the Order. In the Convent, they wore a black robe similarly adorned, with a cap of dignity. The knights were authorised to wear these dresses by a Bull of Pope Alexander IV, in 1259. The other insignia were,—*First*, A star which was worn on the left breast, in the form of a cross patée, having eight points, symbolical of the eight beatitudes and the eight languages, which composed the Order; *Second*, A badge formed of a white enamelled cross, having the angles charged with the supporters, or principal device, of the respective kingdom to which the language belonged. This, surmounted by an imperial Crown, was worn originally suspended from the neck by a gold chain, latterly by a black ribband; to these were added the sword, scarf, spurs, &c. As an armorial distinction, the knights were privileged to augment their family arms with a chief, *gules*, charged with a cross, *argent*; and exteriorly adorned the shield with the mantle, cap of dignity, banners, badge, and motto, *Pro Fide*. These insignia, however, were of more modern adoption.—*Vide* Hospitallaria.

3. The first introduction of the Knights Hospitallers into England took place, according to Tanner, in 1101. Soon after this, the Grand Priory of St. John, at Clerkenwell, London, was founded by the Lord Jordan Briset. In 1185 it was formally dedicated by the Patriarch Heraclius of Jerusalem. Matthew Paris mentions that, in 1237, there went from the Priory of Clerkenwell three hundred knights to the wars in the Holy Land. It was set on fire by the rebels under Wat Tyler in 1381, and burnt for seven days; and it was not finally repaired till one hundred and twenty-three years afterwards, when the Grand Prior Docwra completed its reconstruction. This building is said to have exhibited curious specimens of the Arts of Europe and Asia, and contained collections of books and other rarities.—(Cromwell's Hist. Parish Clerkenwell.)

The old gateway of St. John's, Clerkenwell, is nearly all that remains of the once princely Priory, the revenues of which, at the time of the Reformation, amounted to the sum of two thousand three hundred and eighty-five pounds twelve shillings and eightpence sterling. Besides the above, the Order possessed subordinate priories or establishments in almost every county of England and Scotland; to which were attached valuable lands, with rights of venison and fishing, and immunities of various kinds.

CHAP. II. THE KNIGHTS TEMPLARS.

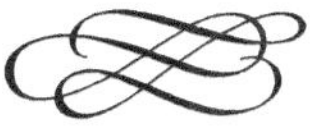

And on his brest a bloodie crosse he bore,
The deare remembrance of his dying Lord,
For whose sweete sake that glorious badge he wore,
And dead, as living, ever him ador'd:
Upon his shield the like was also scor'd,
For soveraine hope, which in his helpe he had,
Right, faithfull, true he was in deede and word:
But of his cheere did seeme too solemne sad;
Yet nothing did he dread, but ever was ydrad."

"AND ON HIS BREST A BLOODIE CROSSE HE BORE,
THE DEARE REMEMBRANCE OF HIS DYING LORD,
FOR WHOSE SWEETE SAKE THAT GLORIOUS BADGE HE
WORE,
AND DEAD, AS LIVING, EVER HIM ADOR'D;
UPON HIS SHIELD THE LIKE WAS ALSO SCOR'D,
FOR SOVERAINE HOPE, WHICH IN HIS HELPE HE HAD.
RIGHT, FAITHFULL, TRUE HE WAS IN DEEDE AND WORD:
BUT OF HIS CHEERE DID SEEME TOO SOLEMNE SAD;
YET NOTHING DID HE DREAD, BUT EVER WAS YDRAD."

*JACQUES DE MOLAY. GRANDE MAITRE DE
L'ORDRE DU TEMPLE.*

It was in the year 1119, the twentieth of the Christian dominion in Syria, that nine pious and valiant Knights, the greater part of whom had been the companions of Godfrey de Bouillon, formed themselves into an association, the object of which was to protect and defend Pilgrims on their visits to the holy places. These Knights, of whom the two chief were Hugo de Payens and Godfrey de St. Omer, vowed, in honour of the *sweet Mother of God*, to unite Monkhood and Knighthood;[1] their pious design met with the warm approbation of the King and the Patriarch, and in the hands of the latter they made the three ordinary vows of poverty, chastity, and obedience; and a fourth, of combating without ceasing against the heathen, in defence of Pilgrims and of the Holy Land; and bound themselves to live according to the rule of the canons of St. Augustine, at Jerusalem. The King assigned them for their abode a part of his palace, which stood close by where had stood the Temple of the Lord. He and his barons contributed to their support, and the abbot and canons of the Temple assigned them for the keeping of their arms and magazines the street between it and the royal palace, and hence they took the name of the soldiery of the Temple, or Templars. When Fulk, Count of Anjou, in the year following the formation of the society, made a pilgrimage to the Holy Land, the Order was even then in such repute that he joined it as a married brother, and on his return home remitted them annually thirty pounds of silver to aid them in their pious labours, and his example was followed by several other Christian princes.

For the first nine years after their institution, the Templars lived in poverty and humility, and no new members joined their society, which was eclipsed by that of St. John. Their clothing consisted of such garments as were bestowed on them by the charity of the faithful, and so rigorously were the gifts of pious princes applied by them to their destination—the benefit of pilgrims and of the Holy Land in general—that in consequence of their poverty, Hugo de Payens and Godfrey de St. Omer had but one war-horse between them. When the Order had arrived at wealth and splendour, its seal, representing two Knights mounted on one charger, commemorated this original poverty of its pious founders.

During the reign of Baldwin II. the kingdom was hard pressed by the Turks of Damascus, Mossul, and the neighbouring states, and the king had been a captive in their hands. On his liberation he sought every means of strengthening his kingdom, and as the Templars had displayed such eminent valour and devotion wherever they had been engaged, he resolved to gain them all the influence and consideration in his power. Accordingly he dispatched two of their members as his envoys to the Holy See, to lay before the Pope the state of the Holy Land, and also furnished them with a strong letter of recommendation to the celebrated Bernard of Clairvaux, the nephew of one of the envoys. Bernard approved highly of the object and institution of the Order. Hugo de Payens and five other brethren soon arrived in the west, and appeared before the fathers, who were assembled in council at Troyes, to whom Hugo detailed the maxims and the deeds of the Templars. The fathers expressed their approbation of all he said, the Order was pronounced good and useful, and same additions, taken from that of the Benedictines, were made to their rule. By the direction of Pope Honorius, the council appointed them a white mantle as their peculiar dress, to which Pope Eugenius some years afterwards added a red cross on the breast—the symbol of martyrdom. Their banner was of the black and white stripe, called, in old French, *Bauseant* (which word became their war-cry,) and bore the pious inscription, *Non nobis, Domine, non nobis, sed nomini tua da gloriam.*[2] St. Bernard, if he did not himself draw up the rule of Order, had at least a considerable participation in it; throughout his life he cherished the Templars; he rarely wrote a letter to the Holy Land, in which he did not praise them, and recommend them to the favour and protection of the great.

Owing to the influence of Bernard, and the sincere piety and noble qualities of its founders, the Order rapidly increased in wealth and consequence. Many Knights assumed its habit, and with Hugo de Payens travelled through France and England, to excite the Christians to the sacred war. With Henry I. of England they met the highest consideration. Fulk, of Anjou, re-united himself to Hugo de Payens, and on the invitation of King Baldwin, prepared, though advanced in years, to set out for Palestine, to espouse the daughter of the king, and succeed him on his throne. Gifts in abundance flowed in on the Order, large possessions were bestowed on it in all countries of the west, and Hugo de Payens, now its Grand Master, returned to the Holy Land in the year 1129, at the head of three hundred Knights Templars of the noblest families in Europe, ready to take the field against the Infidels.

The Templars soon became, in fact, the most distinguished of the Christian warriors. By a rule of their Order, no brother could be redeemed for a higher ransom than a girdle or a knife, or some such trifle;[3] captivity was therefore equivalent to death, and they always fought with Spartan desperation. The Bauseant was always in the thick of the battle; the revenue they enjoyed enabled them to draw to their standard valiant secular knights and stout and hardy footmen. The chivalry of St. John vied with them, it is true, in prowess and valour, but they do not occupy the same space in the History of the Crusades. The Templars having been from the outset solely devoted to arms,—the warm interest which St. Bernard, whose influence was so great, took in their welfare,— and the circumstance that the fourth King of Jerusalem was a member of their body,—all combined to throw a splendour about them which the Knights of St. John could not claim, but which also gave occasion to their more speedy corruption, and augmented the number of their enemies. Most writers, however, of the twelfth century speak respectfully of the Knights of the Temple, and those unsparing satirists, the Troubadours, never mention them but with honour. The history of the Order, as far as we can recollect, records only one instance of a Templar abjuring his faith, and that was an English Knight, Robert of Saint Albans, who deserted to Saladin, who gave him his sister in marriage on his becoming a Moslem; and in 1185, the ex-red-cross Knight led a Saracen army to the neighbourhood of Jerusalem, wasting and destroying the country with fire and sword.[4]

By the Bull, *Omne datum optimum*, granted by Pope Alexander III. in 1162, the Order of the Templars acquired great importance, and from this time forth, it may be regarded as totally independent, acknowledging no authority but that—before which the haughtiest monarchs bowed—of the supreme pontiff, who protected and favoured them as his champions against all who might dispute his will. It is therefore of importance to look at its constitution, and what were its revenues and possessions.

The Order of the Templars consisted of three distinct *classes*, not *degrees*—knights, chaplains, and service-brethren, to which may be added those who were attached to the Order under the name of *affiliated*, *donates*, and *oblates*.[5] The strength and flower of the Order were the Knights; all its dignities and superior offices belonged to them. The candidate for admission among the Knights of the Temple was required to produce proof of his being the lawful issue of a Knight, or of one qualified to receive that distinction; and he must himself have already received the honour-conferring blow from a Secular Knight, for the Order was Spiritual, and, as members, could not deign to accept honour from a layman. The only exception was in the case of a bishop, who might draw his sword among the brethren of the Temple, without having been a secular Knight. The aspirant must moreover be free from debt, and, on admission, pay a considerable sum into the hands of the society.[6] The most unlimited obedience to the commands of his superiors in the house and in the field of battle; the total abnegation of all interests but those of the society, (for the Templar could hold no property, could receive no private letter); the most unflinching valour, (for so long as a Christian banner waved in the field, the Templar, however severely wounded, must not abandon it),—were the duties of the Knights of the Temple. If he fled, disgrace and punishment awaited him; if he surrendered, he had to end his life amid the torments inflicted by the enraged Moslems, or to languish in perpetual captivity, for the Order never redeemed its members. Hence, then, the Templar was valiant as the fabled heroes of romance; hence prodigies of prowess, such as almost surpass belief, so frequently illustrate the name of the soldiers of the Temple. Every motive that could stimulate to deeds of renown combined to actuate the soldier-monk A Knight, he obeyed the call of honour and emulation; a Monk, (but the Templar was not, as some erroneously fancy, a Priest), he was, according to the ideas of the times, engaged in the service most acceptable to God.

The mode of reception into the Order corresponded with the dignity and importance of the character of a Knight Templar. Though a noviciate was enjoined by the original canons, in practice it was dispensed with; the candidate was, after all due inquiry had been made, received in a chapter assembled in the chapel of the Order. All strangers, even the relatives of the aspirant, were excluded. The preceptor (usually one of the priors) opened the business with an address to those present, calling on them to declare if they knew of any just cause and impediment to the aspirant, whom the majority had agreed to receive, becoming a member of their body.[7] If all were silent, the candidate was led into an adjacent chamber, whither two or three of the Knights came to him, and setting before him the rigour and strictness of the Order, inquired if he still persisted in his desire to enter it. If he did persist, they inquired if he was married or betrothed; had made a vow in any other Order; if he owed more than he could pay; if he was of sound body, without any secret infirmity, and free? If his answers proved satisfactory, they left him and returned to the chapter, and the preceptor again asked if any one had anything to say against his being received. If all were silent, he asked if they were willing to admit him. On their assenting, the candidate was led in by the Knights who had questioned him, and who now instructed him in the mode of asking admission. He advanced, kneeling, with folded hands, before the preceptor, and said, "Sir, I am come before God, and before you and the brethren; and I pray and beseech you, for the sake of God and our sweet lady, to receive me into your society and the good works of the Order, as one who, all his life long, will be the servant and slave of the Order." The preceptor then questioned him, if he had well considered all the toils and difficulties which awaited him in the Order, adjured him on the Holy Evangelists to speak the truth, then put to him the questions already asked by the Knights, farther inquiring if he was a Knight, the son of a Knight and a gentlewoman, and if he was a priest. He then asked if he would promise to God and Mary, our dear lady, obedience, as long as he lived, to the Master of the Temple, and the prior who should be set over him; chastity of his body; [8] compliance with the laudable manners and customs of the Order then in force, and such as the Master and Knights might hereafter add; fight for and defend, with all his might, the holy land of Jerusalem; never quit the Order but with consent of the Master and the Chapter; never see a Christian unjustly deprived of his inheritance, or be aiding in such deed. The preceptor then said—"In the name, then, of God and of Mary, our dear lady, and in the name of St. Peter of Rome, and of our father the Pope, and in the name of all the brethren of the Temple, we receive you to all the good works of the Order, which have been performed from the beginning, and will be performed to the end, you, your father, your mother, and all those of your family whom you let participate therein. So you, in like manner, receive us to all the good works which you have performed and will perform. We assure you of bread and water, the poor clothing of the Order, and labour and toil enow." The preceptor then took the white mantle, with its ruddy cross, placed it about his neck, and bound it fast. The chaplain repeated the one hundred and thirty-second Psalm, *Ecce quam bonum*, and the prayer of the Holy Spirit, *Deus qui corda fidelium*, each brother said a *Pater*, the preceptor kissed the new brother, the chaplain did the same. The Templar then placed himself at the feet of the preceptor, and was by him exhorted to peace and charity with his brother Christians; to chastity, obedience, humility, and piety; and thus the ceremony ended.

At the head of the Order stood the Grand Master, who, like the General of the Jesuits in modern times, was independent of all authority but that of the sovereign pontiff. The residence of the Grand Master was the city of Jerusalem; when the city was lost, he fixed his seat at Antioch, next at Acre, then at the castle of the Pilgrims,[9] between Caiphas and Cæsarea, and finally in Cyprus, for his duty required him to be always in the Holy Land. The Grand Master never resided in Europe until the time of Jacques de Molay. The power of the Grand Master was considerable, though he was very much controuled by the chapter, without whose consent he could not dispose of any of the higher offices, or undertake any thing of importance. He could not, for instance, take money out of the treasury, without the consent of the prior of Jerusalem; he could neither make war or truce, or alter laws, but with the approbation of the chapter. But the Grand Master had the right of bestowing the small commands, the governments of houses of the Order, and of selecting the brethren who should form the chapter, which power was again controuled by there being always assigned him two brethren as assistants, who, with the Seneschal, were to form a part of every chapter. The Order was aristocratic rather than monarchic; the Grand Master was like a Doge of Venice, and his real power chiefly depended on his personal qualities; he had, however, many distinctions; the greater part of the executive power was in his hands—in war he was the commander-in-chief; he had, as vicar-general of the Pope, episcopal jurisdiction over the clergy of the Order; he ranked with princes, and his establishment corresponded thereto; he had for his service four horses, a chaplain, two secretaries, a squire of noble birth, a farrier, a Turcopole and cook, with footmen, and a Turcoman for a guide, who was usually fastened by a cord to prevent his escape. When the Grand Master died, his funeral was celebrated with great solemnity by the light of torches and wax tapers,—an honour bestowed by the Order on no other of its Members. All the Knights and Prelates were invited to assist. Each Brother who was present was to repeat two hundred *Pater Nosters* within the space of seven days, for the repose of the soul of the deceased;

and one hundred poor persons were fed at home, at the expense of the Order, with the same design. [10]

Each province of the Order had a Grand Prior, who represented in it the Grand Master; each house had its Prior at its head, who commanded its Knights in war, and presided over its chapters in peace. In England, the Grand Prior sat in Parliament as a Peer of the Realm. To complete this sketch of the Order, we may remark, that except Scandinavia, (for they had some possessions in Hungary,) there was not a country in Europe in which the lavish piety of princes and nobles had not bestowed on the Templars a considerable portion of the wealth of the state; for in every province the Order had its churches and chapels—the number of which was in the year 1240, as great as 1050—villages, farm-houses, mills, corn-lands, pastures, woods, rights of venison, and fisheries. [11] The revenues of the Templars in England in 1185, as given by Dugdale, will afford some idea of their wealth. The entire annual income of the Order has been estimated at not less than six millions sterling.

It cannot be denied, that this enormous wealth, together with the luxury and other evils which it engendered, provoked the hatred of the secular clergy and laity, and paved the way to the spoliation of the Order. In 1252, the pious pope-ridden Henry III. of England said, that the prelates and clergy in general, but especially the Templars and Hospitallers, had so many liberties and privileges, that their excessive wealth made them mad with pride; he added, that what had been bestowed imprudently, ought to be prudently resumed, and declared his intention of revoking the inconsiderate grants of himself and his predecessors. The Grand Prior of the Templars replied, "What sayest thou, my Lord the King? Far be it that so discourteous and absurd a word should be uttered by thy mouth. So long as thou observest justice, thou mayest be a king, and as soon as thou infringest it, thou wilt cease to be a king." A bold expression certainly, but the Prior knew his man well, and he would hardly have spoken so to the son of Henry. The anecdote of Richard I. bestowing his daughter Pride in marriage on the Templars, is well known; and numerous traits of their haughtiness, avarice, luxury, and other of the current vices, may be found in the writers of the thirteenth century; but till the final attack was made, no worse charge was brought against them, unless such is implied in a bull of Pope Clement IV. in 1265, which is, however, easily capable of a milder interpretation. Mr. Raynouard asserts, too, that the proverbial expression *bibere Templariter* is used by no writer of the thirteenth century. In this he is preceded by Baluze and Roquefort, who maintain, that, like *bibere Papaliter*, it only signified to live in abundance and comfort.

---

1. The other original associates of the Order were the Knights Roral, Gundemar, Godfrey Bisol, Payens de Montidier, Archibald de St. Aman, Andrew de Montbar, and the Count of Provence, according to the German historian, Wilcke.

2. *Bauseant* or *Bausant*, was, in old French, a pie-bald horse. The word is still preserved with its original meaning in the Scotch dialect, in the form *Bawsent*:—

   "His honest, sonsie, baws'nt face,

   Aye gat him freends in ilka place,"

   says Burns, describing the "Ploughman's Collie" in his Tale of the "Twa Dogs;" and in the Glossary, Dr. Currie explains *Bawsent* as meaning "having a white stripe down the face." Some conceive that the word *Beauseant* may be merely an old variation of the modern French word *Bienséant*, as referring to something handsome or attractive.

3. Expediency afterwards prompted the infraction of this original rule. Gerard de Ridefort, Grand Master of the Order, was liberated by Saladin, along with several other captives, for no less a ransom than the city of Ascalon. In 1244 also, the Templars endeavoured to redeem their brethren from captivity in Egypt.

4. Mathew Paris charges a certain Templar, named Ferrandus, with having gone over to the Infidels, and betrayed the state of the Christian garrison in Damietta, A. D. 1221. This deserter was reputed to have been a knight "*in armis strenuus et consilio circumspectus.*"

5. The *affiliated* were persons of various ranks, and of both sexes, who, without any outward sign of connection, were acknowledged by the Order as entitled to its protection, and admitted to a participation in certain of its privileges,—such as exemption

from the effects of ecclesiastical interdicts, which secured to them at least the occasional service of the mass, and Christian burial in consecrated ground. These were advantages of the last importance, for which both men and women, Knights and Burghers, were content to pay considerable sums while alive, and leave to the Treasury of the Temple the residue of their property after death.

The *donates* and *oblates* stood in a somewhat different relation to the Order, being personally dedicated or offered, as their titles denote, to the Society. These were either youths whom their parents destined for the service of the Order, when they had attained a proper age, or they were adults who bound themselves gratuitously to aid and assist the Order so long as they lived, solely in admiration of its sanctity and excellence, a portion of which they humbly hoped to share. Among these latter, all classes were to be found,—princes and priests, as well as other persons. (See Secret Societies of the Middle Ages.)

6. No specific sum appears to have been exacted from entrants, but each was expected to pay according to his means. Thus it is recorded of the Prince Guy Dauphin, that he gave to the Order 1500 pieces (Livr. Tourn.) for his own entry-money, and a contribution of 200 a-year in name of his parents.

Wealthy Squires of the Order, of respectable though not noble parentage, gave sometimes large sums at their reception. Of this class, Bartholomew Bartholet gave property to the amount of 1,000 livres Tournois to be admitted, and William of Liege gave 200 a-year of the same circulation.

7. Hugo de Payens, the founder of the Order, set a laudable example of rigour in the selection of candidates. When a certain Knight, named Hugo d'Amboise, was desirous of being received into the Order, the Grand Master refused to let him take the vows, because he had oppressed the people of Marmoutier, and disobeyed a judicial sentence of the Count of Anjou; and until he had given satisfaction to all whom he had injured, and otherwise amended his life, he was informed that he could not be admitted into the Temple.

8. The Rule of St. Bernard prohibited the Templars from even looking at a woman. The translation of the statute, chap. lxxii, is as follows:—

"We hold it to be dangerous to all religion to look too much on the countenance of women, and, therefore, let no Brother presume to kiss either widow or virgin, or mother or sister, or aunt, or any other woman. Let the militia of Christ, therefore, shun feminine kisses, by which men are often exposed to danger, that with a pure conscience and secure life, they may walk continually in the sight of God."

 9. This stronghold of the Order was built about 1217, under the Grand Master, William de Chartres, who employed a number of pilgrims of the masonic class in its erection. Hence the appellation of Pilgrim Castle which it received.

10. The Knights in general seem to have been buried with their swords placed beside the body. Several skeletons are said to have been found in the Templar Cemetery at Mount Hooly, near Edinburgh, lying cross-legged, with swords by their sides. See Maitland's History of Edinburgh.

11. The first preceptory of the Templars in England was founded at Holborn, then in the suburbs of London, whence they afterwards removed to Fleet Street about 1185. The only remains of the latter place of residence is the beautiful circular edifice still called the Temple Church, supposed to have been built after the model of the Church of the Holy Sepulchre at Jerusalem. This seems to have been a favourite form with the Order. The Church of St. Sepulchre at Cambridge, built by the Templars, is of a circular construction, having the appearance of a fortified tower. In examining this building (says Mr. Britton) we are struck with its ponderous and durable appearance, as if it was intended for a castellated edifice. The masonry of the ancient walls, and also of the pillars and arches, is such as to evince great skill in the building, the stones being all squared and chisselled with the most perfect accuracy to fit their respective places. At Northampton, the same form seems to have been observed. The Church of the Holy Sepulchre (says Pennant, speaking of this place,) was supposed to have been built by the Knights Templars on the model of that at Jerusalem. Others of the chapels appertaining to the Order do not, however, present a similar plan.

The principal Bailliwicks of the Order in England were the following, viz. London, Kent, Warwick, Waesdone, Lincoln, Lindsey, Bolingbroke, Widine, Agerstone, York. In these were seventeen preceptories. Most places having the prefix of *Temple* belonged to the Knights,—such as Temple-Bruer in Lincolnshire, where, Camden says, that in his time there were the ruins of a church or chapel, "not unlike that of the new Temple at London." Probably it was of the circular form above noticed. Some account of the Irish preceptories will be found in the Appendix.

CHAP. III. THE PERSECUTION OF THE TEMPLARS.

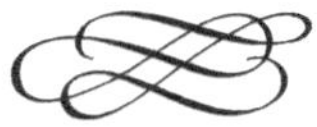

When Acre fell in 1292, the Templars, having lost all their possessions and a great number of their members in the Holy Land, retired with the other Christians to Cyprus. Having probably seen the folly of all hope of recovering the Holy Land, they grew indifferent about it; few members joined them from Europe, and it is more than probable that they meditated a removal of the chief seat of the Order to France.[1] The Hospitallers, on the other hand, with more prudence, as events showed, resolved to continue the war against the infidels, and they attacked and conquered Rhodes; while the Teutonic knights transferred the sphere of their pious warfare to Prussia against its heathen inhabitants. Thus, while the Templars were falling under the reproach of being luxurious Knights, their rivals rose in consideration, and there was an active and inveterate enemy ready to take advantage of their ill-repute.

Philip the Fair, a tyrannical and rapacious prince, was at that time on the throne of France. His darling object was to set the power of the monarchy above that of the church. In his celebrated controversy with Pope Boniface, the Templars had been on the side of the Holy See. Philip, whose animosity pursued Boniface even beyond the grave, wished to be revenged on all who had taken his side; moreover, the immense wealth of the Templars, which he reckoned on making his own if he could destroy them, strongly attracted the king, who had already tasted of the sweets of the spoliation of the Lombards and the Jews; and he probably, also, feared the obstacle to the perfect establishment of despotism which might be offered by a numerous, noble, and wealthy society, such as the Templars formed. Boniface's successor, Clement V. was the creature of Philip, to whom he owed his dignity, and at his accession had bound himself to the performance of six articles in favour of Philip, one of which was not expressed. It was probably inserted without any definite object, and intended to serve the interest of the French monarch on any occasion which might present itself.

LA TOUR DU TEMPLE À PARIS

It had been the object of Pope Boniface to form the three Military Orders into one, and he had summoned them to Rome for that purpose, but his death prevented it. Clement, on this, June 6, 1306, addressed the Grand Masters of the Templars and the Hospitallers, inviting them to come to consult with him about the best mode of supporting the Kings of Armenia and Cyprus. He desired them to come as secretly as possible, and with a very small train, as they would find abundance of their Knights this side the sea; and he directed them to provide for the defence of Limisso in Cyprus during their short absence. Fortunately perhaps for himself and his Order, the Master of the Hospitallers was then engaged in the conquest of Rhodes, but Jacques de Molay,[2] the Master of the Templars, immediately prepared to obey the mandate of the Pope, and he left Cyprus with a train of 60 Knights, and a treasure of 150,000 florins of gold, and a great quantity of silver money, the whole requiring twelve horses to carry it.[3] He proceeded to Paris, where he was received with the greatest honours by the King, and he deposited his treasure in the Temple of that city. It is, as we have said, not impossible that it was the intention of Molay to transfer the chief seat of the Order thither, and that he had, therefore, brought with him its treasure and the greater part of the members of the chapter; and indeed it is difficult to say how early the project of attacking the Templars entered into the minds of Philip and his obsequious lawyers, or whether he originally aimed at more than mulcting them under the pretext of reformation: and farther, whether the first informers against them were suborned or not. The records leave a considerable degree of obscurity on the whole matter. All we can learn is, that a man named Squin de Flexian, who had been a Prior of the Templars, and had been expelled the Order for heresy and various vices, was lying in prison at Paris or Toulouse, it is uncertain which. In the prison with him was a Florentine named Noffo Dei, "a man," says Villani, "full of all iniquity." These two began to plan how they might extricate themselves from the confinement to which they seemed perpetually doomed. The example of the process against the memory of Pope Boniface, shewed them that no lie was too gross or absurd not to obtain ready credence, and they fixed on the Templars as the objects of their charges. Squin told the governor of the prison that he had a communication to make to the King, which would be of more value to him than if he had gained a kingdom, but that he would only tell it to the King in person. He was brought to Philip, who promised him his life, and he made his confession, on which the King immediately arrested some of the Templars, who are said to have confirmed the truth of Squin's assertions. Shortly afterwards, it is said, similar discoveries were made to the Pope by his chamberlain, Cardinal Cantilupo, who had been in connexion with the Templars from his eleventh year.

Squin Flexian declared,

1. That every member on admission into the Order swore on all occasions to defend its interests right or wrong;

2. That the heads of the Order were in secret confederacy with the Saracens, had more of Mahommedan unbelief than of Christian faith, as was proved by the mode of reception into the Order, when the novice was made to spit and trample on the crucifix, and blaspheme the faith of Christ;

3. That the superiors were sacrilegious, cruel, and

heretical murderers; for if any novice, disgusted with its profligacy, wished to quit the Order, they secretly murdered him, and buried him by night; so, also, when women were pregnant by them, they taught them how to produce abortion, or secretly put the infants to death;

4. The Templars were addicted to the error of the Fraticelli, and, like them, despised the authority of the Pope and the Church;

5. That the superiors were addicted to the practice of horrible crimes, and if any one opposed them, they were condemned by the Master to perpetual imprisonment;

6. That their houses were the abode of every vice and iniquity;

7. That they endeavoured to put the Holy Land into the hands of the Saracens, whom they favoured more than the Christians. Three other articles of less importance completed this first body of charges. It is remarkable, that we do not find among them those which made such a figure in the subsequent examinations; namely, the devil appearing among them in the shape of a cat; their idolatrous worship of an image with one or three heads, or a skull covered with human skin, with carbuncles for eyes, before which they burned the bodies of their dead brethren, and then mingled the ashes with their drink, thereby thinking to gain more courage; and, finally, their smearing this idol with human fat.[4]

It was unfortunate for the Templars that their chapters were held in secret,[5] and by night, for an opportunity was thereby afforded to their enemies of laying whatever secret enormities they pleased to their charge, to refute which, by the production of indifferent witnesses, was consequently out of their power. Philip having now all things prepared, sent, like his descendant Charles IX. previous to the St. Bartholomew massacre, secret orders to all his governors to arm themselves on the 12th of October, and on the following night, but not sooner, on pain of death, to open the king's letter, and act according to it. On Friday the 13th of October, all the Templars throughout France were simultaneously arrested at break of day. The unhappy Knights were thrown into cold cheerless dungeons, (for they were arrested, we should remember, at the commencement of winter), had barely the necessaries of life, were deprived of the habit of their Order, and of the rites and comforts of the church; were exposed to every species of torture then in use, were shown a real or pretended letter of the Grand Master, in which he confessed several of the charges, and exhorted them to do the same; and finally, were promised life and liberty, if they freely acknowledged the guilt of the Order. Can we then be surprised that the spirit of many a Knight was broken, that any hope of escape from misery was eagerly caught at, and that falsehoods, the most improbable, were declared to be true? And it is remarkable that the most improbable charges are those which were most frequently acknowledged, so just is the observation, that men will more readily in such circumstances acknowledge what is false than what is true; for the false they know can be afterwards refuted by its own absurdity, whereas truth is permanent.

Of the Templars in England 228 were examined;[6] the Dominican, Carmelite, Minorite, and Augustinian friars brought abundance of hearsay evidence against them, but nothing of any importance was proved; in Castile and Leon it was the same; in Aragon the Knights bravely endured the torture, and maintained their innocence; in Germany all the lay witnesses testified in their favour; in Italy their enemies were more successful, as the influence of the Pope was there considerable, yet in Lombardy the Bishops acquitted the Knights. Charles of Anjou, the cousin of Philip, and the foe of the Templars, who had sided with Frederick against him, could not fail, it may be supposed, in getting some evidences of their guilt in Sicily, Naples, and Provence. It is not undeserving of attention, that one of these witnesses, who had been received into the Order in Catalonia, (where all who were examined had declared the innocence of the Order), said he had been received there in the usual impious and indecent manner, and mentioned the appearance and the worship of the cat in the chapter!! Such is the value of rack-extorted testimony! In fine, in every country out of the sphere of the immediate influence of Clement, Philip, and Charles, the general innocence of the Order was acknowledged. In Portugal they were preserved under the altered appellation of the Knights of Christ,—a change which was effected by the friendly policy of Prince Denys, who in 1218, secured for them the sanction of the successor of Clement.[7]

Throughout the entire process against the Templars, from October 1307 to May 1312, the most determined design of the King and his ministers to destroy the Order meets us at every step; Philip would have blood to justify robbery; several Templars had already expired on the rack, perished from the rigour of their imprisonment, or died by their own hands; but on the 12th May 1310, fifty-four Templars who had confessed, but afterwards retracted, were by his order committed to the flames, in Paris, as relapsed heretics. They endured with heroic constancy the most cruel tortures, asserting with their latest breath the innocence of the Order, though offered life if they would confess, and implored to do so by their friends and relatives. Similar executions took place in other towns. The Pope soon went heart and hand with Philip. In vain did the bishops assembled at Vienne propose to hear those members who came forward as the defenders of the Order. A Bull of the Pope was fulminated against the Order,[8] and transferred its possessions to the Knights of St. John, who, however, had to pay such enormous fines to the King and Pope before they could enter on them, as almost ruined them; so that if Philip did not succeed to the utmost of his anticipations, he had little reason to complain of his share.[9] The members of the society of the Templars were permitted to enter that of the Hospitallers, —a strange indulgence for those that had spitten on the cross, and practised horrible vices.

But the atrocious scene was yet to come which was to complete the ruin of the Templars, and satiate the vengeance of their enemies. Their Grand Master, Molay, and three other dignitaries of the Order, still survived: And, though they had made the most submissive acknowledgments to their unrelenting persecutors, yet the influence which they had over the minds of the vulgar, and their connection with many of the Princes of Europe, rendered them formidable and dangerous to their oppressors. By the exertion of that influence, they might restore union to their dismembered party, and inspire them with courage to revenge the murder of their companions;[10] or, by adopting a more cautious method, they might repel, by uncontrovertible proofs, the charges for which they suffered; and, by interesting all men in their behalf, they might expose Philip to the attacks of his own subjects, and to the hatred and contempt of Europe. Aware of the dangers to which his character and person would be exposed by pardoning the surviving Templars, the French Monarch commanded the Grand Master and his Brethren to be led out to a scaffold, erected for the purpose, and there to confess before the public, the enormities of which their Order had been guilty, and the justice of the punishment which had been inflicted on their brethren. If they adhered to their former confession, a full pardon was promised to them; but if they should persist in maintaining their innocence, they were threatened with destruction on a pile of wood, which the executioners had erected in their view, to awe them into compliance. While the multitude were standing around in awful expectation, ready, from the words of the prisoners, to justify or condemn their King, the venerable Molay, with a cheerful and undaunted countenance, advanced, in chains, to the edge of the scaffold; and, with a firm and impressive tone, thus addressed the spectators.—"It is but just, that in this terrible day, and in the last moments of my life, I lay open the iniquity of falsehood, and make truth to triumph. I declare then, in the face of heaven and earth, and I confess, though to my eternal shame and confusion, that I have committed the greatest of crimes; but it has been only in acknowledging those that have been charged with so much virulence upon an Order, which truth obliges me to pronounce innocent. I made the first declaration they required of me, only to suspend the excessive tortures of the rack, and mollify those that made me endure them. I am sensible what torments they prepare for those that have courage to revoke such a confession. But the horrible sight which they present to my eyes, is not capable of making me confirm one lie by another. On a condition so infamous as that, I freely renounce life, which is already but too odious to me. For what would it avail me to prolong a few miserable days, when I must owe them only to the blackest of calumnies."[11] In consequence of this manly revocation, the Grand Master and his companions were hurried into the flames, where they retained that contempt for death which they had exhibited on former occasions. This mournful scene extorted tears

40

from the lowest of the vulgar.[12] Four valiant Knights, whose charity and valour had procured them the gratitude and applause of mankind, suffering, without fear, the most cruel and ignominious death, was, indeed, a spectacle well calculated to excite emotions of pity in the hardest hearts. Humanity shudders at the recital of the horrid deed; and if the voice of impartial posterity has not, with one accord, pronounced the unqualified acquittal of the Templars, it has branded with the mark of eternal infamy the conduct of their accusers and judges.

---

1. This seems somewhat countenanced by the great additions made to the buildings of the Temple at Paris previous to the arrival of the Grand Master. In 1306, was erected a large square tower, flanked by four round towers, with an adjacent building on the north side, surmounted by turrets. The principal tower contained four stories, in each of which there was an apartment thirty feet square: three of the inferior towers had also each a hall. The remaining tower contained a fine staircase, which conducted to the different chambers and battlements. The walls of the central keep were nine feet in thickness. This *Tower of the Temple* has been rendered memorable in modern times by the captivity of the unfortunate Louis XVI. and his family. It is also noted as the place of imprisonment, by Buonaparte, of the celebrated Sir Sidney Smith, now the Head of the Order of the Temple.
2. Jacques de Molay was elected Grand Master in the year 1297, and was the second elevated to that dignity after the expulsion of the Christians from the Holy Land. He was of an ancient family in Besançon, Franche Compté, and entered the Order in the year 1265.
3. It is probable that part of this treasure was formed from the spoils of Greece, which the Templars had been invited from their retirement to invade, at the instigation of the King of Sicily. After overrunning great part of that country, they re-

turned loaded with the plunder of its cities, leaving their possession to some allies.—*Vide Michaud, Histoire des Croisades.*

4. A French writer gives the following opinion regarding the origin of some of these charges:—"Les Chevaliers supportaient un grand nombre d'épreuves religieuses et morales avant de parvenir aux divers degrés d'initiation; ainsi, par exemple, le récipiendaire pouvait recevoir l'injonction, sous peine de mort, de fouler aux pieds le crucifix, ou d'adorer une idole; mais, s'il cédait à la terreur qu'on cherchait à lui inspirer, il était déclaré indigne d'être admis aux grades élevés de l'Ordre. On conçoit, d'après cela, comment des êtres, trop faibles ou trop immoraux pour supporter les épreuves d'initiation, ont pu accuser les Templiers de se livrer a des practiques et d'avoir des croyances infâmes, superstitieuses."—(Recherches Historiques sur Les Templiers. Paris, 1835.)

5. "Quod clam consueverunt tenere capitula sua;" and "Quod similem clandestinitatem observant et observare consueverunt ut plurimum in recipiendo fratres," were principal counts in the indictment against them. From this secrecy, some writers have inferred that the Templars practised a species of Freemasonry, of which certainly no direct evidence transpired during the inquest. Signor Rosetti, the celebrated commentator of Dante, has, we understand, a work in the press, in which he seeks to demonstrate that the Templars were a branch of that great secret confederacy which was formed against the papacy, which included the Troubadours and all the *literati* of the time, and which ultimately produced the Reformation. This information is derived from a letter to Dr. Burnes by Mr. Keightly, the talented reviewer and friend of Rosetti.

6. In June 1310, Pope Clement wrote to the King of England blaming his lenity, and calling upon him to employ the torture upon the unfortunate Knights. The Council of London, after a long discussion, ordered it to be employed, but so as not to mutilate the limbs, or cause an incurable wound, or violent effusion of blood.

7. The Knights of Christ have continued to exist as a recognized Order of Knighthood down to the present day. The supremacy is vested in the Sovereign of Portugal, and the greater part of the revenue is understood to accrue to the royal coffers. The sums, however, paid in pensions to Knights of the Order, about the beginning of the present century, are said to have amounted to about £4000 per annum. In 1793 they possessed twenty-one provincial towns and villages, and counted four

hundred and fifty-four commanderies, exclusive of colonial acquisitions. The various recent changes, occasioned by war and intestine commotions, probably have reduced their income and possessions. In 1820 the Grand Prior of Portugal was Louis Antonio de Fontado, of the House of Barbasena, and who died in 1832. We are not informed as to his successor. The Cross of the Order of Christ is sometimes bestowed upon foreigners as an honorary distinction. Dr. Bowring, (who was employed on a mission to the Portuguese Government,) and several other Englishmen, have of late years received its Cross; generally, it is believed, that of the third class of Knights.

8. The Pope (Clement V.) committed the glaring absurdity of making a provisional decree to be executed in perpetuity. The Bull which is issued at the Court at Vienne, without asking the judgment of the assembled bishops and others, declares, that although he cannot of right, consistently with the Inquisition and proceedings, pronounce a definite sentence, yet by way of apostolical provision and regulation, he perpetually prohibited people from entering into the Order, and calling themselves Templars. The penalty of the greater excommunication was held out as a punishment for offending.

   Mills' Chivalry, Vol. I. Chap. 7.

   An extract from the Bull, in the original Latin, will be found in the Appendix.

9. Besides appropriating to himself all the moveable property of the Order, three hundred thousand livres of France were retained by the King, ostensibly to repay the expense of the prosecution. No doubt the treasure brought by De Molay from Cyprus would be amongst the first booty seized, as well as the rich gold and silver utensils and plate, with which the chapel and palace of the Temple at Paris were furnished.

10. On the 28th March 1310, no fewer than 546 Templars were assembled under a strong guard, in the gardens of the Bishop of Paris, who had been conveyed thither to make the defence of the Order, and hear read the accusations against them. This shew of justice was, of course, a mere pretence of their persecutors, to save appearances. The number of the Templars in Paris afterwards encreased to nearly 900. Ferrati of Vicenza has reckoned the entire members of the Order throughout Europe at 15,000 persons.

11. Histoire des Chevaliers Hospitaliers de Saint Jean de Jerusalem, par l'Abbe Vertot, tom. ii. pp. 101, 102.

12. So dreadful and impressive an event could not fail to be the source of many strange stories with the vulgar. Among these, chroniclers report, that the venerable martyr, ere life was extinct, summoned Pope Clement to answer before the bar of the Almighty Judge, within forty days, and King Philip before the same tribunal, within the space of a year. Certain it is, that the Pope did suddenly die in the night between the 19th and 20th of the following month; and the church in which his body was placed taking fire, one-half of the corpse was consumed,—a circumstance which naturally confirmed the people in the belief that his death was a special judgment of Heaven for the burning of the knights, and which probably also suggested the prediction. In the month of July following, a tumult arose in the town where the half consumed corpse was kept, during which the populace tried to get forcible possession of the remains; but whether from some superstitious motive, or with a view of avenging on the Pope's body the murder of De Molay, is not known. Philip of France expired within the year, in consequence of a fall from his horse, and others of the persecutors of the Order met a violent death.

CHAP. IV. THE CONTINUATION OF THE ORDER.

But the persecution of the Templars in the fourteenth century does not close the history of the Order; for, though the Knights were spoliated, the Order was not annihilated. In truth, the cavaliers were not guilty,—the brother hood was not suppressed,—and, startling as is the assertion, there has been a succession of Knights Templars from the twelfth century down even to these days; the chain of transmission is perfect in all its links. Jacques de Molay, the Grand Master at the time of the persecution, anticipating his own martyrdom, appointed as his successor, in power and dignity, Johannes Marcus Larmenius of Jerusalem, and from that time to the present there has been a regular and uninterrupted line of Grand Masters. The charter[1] by which the supreme authority has been transmitted, is judicial and conclusive evidence of the Order's continued existence. The charter of transmission, with the signatures of the various chiefs of the Temple, is still preserved at Paris, with the ancient statutes of the Order, the rituals, the records, the seals, the standards, and other memorials of the early Templars.

BERTRAND DU GUESCLIN From a Wood-cut in
a rare gothic folio, printed at Lyons, 1490,
preserved in the Bibliothèque Royale, Paris; and
called the "Chronique de Bertrand du Guesclin."

The brotherhood has been headed by the bravest cavaliers of France, by men who, jealous of the digni-

46

ties of Knighthood, would admit no corruption, no base copies of the orders of chivalry, and who thought that the shield of their nobility was enriched by the impress of the Templars' red cross. Bertrand du Guesclin was the Grand Master from 1357 till his death in 1380, and he was the only French commander who prevailed over the chivalry of our Edward III. From 1478 to 1497, we may mark Robert Lenoncourt, a cavalier of one of the most ancient and valiant families of Lorraine. Phillippe Chabot, a renowned captain in the reign of Francis I., wielded the staff of power from 1516 to 1543. The illustrious family of Montmorency appear as Knights Templars, and Henry, the first Duke, was the chief of the Order from the year 1574 to 1614. At the close of the seventeenth century, the Grand Master was James Henry de Duras, a marshal of France, the nephew of Turenne, and one of the most skilful soldiers of Louis XIV. The Grand Masters from 1724 to 1776 were three princes of the royal Bourbon family. The names and years of power of these royal personages who acknowledged the dignity of the Order of the Temple, were Louis Augustus Bourbon, Duke of Maine, 1724-1737,—Louis Henry Bourbon Conde, 1737-1741,—and Louis Francis Bourbon Conty, 1741-1746. The successor of these princes in the Grand Mastership of the Temple was Louis Hercules Timoleon, Duke de Cosse Brissac, the descendant of an ancient family long celebrated in French history for its loyalty and gallant bearing. He accepted the office in 1776, and sustained it till he died in the cause of royalty at the beginning of the French Revolution. The Order has now at its head Sir William Sidney Smith, of chivalric renown, who became Regent upon the death of the late Grand Master, Bernard Raymond Fabré Palaprat. The high and heroic character of Sir Sidney Smith,—[2] whose deeds of arms at St. Jean d'Acre, rivalling those of the Royal Crusader, Richard I, obtained for him by Eastern Nations the appellation of the modern "Cœur de Lion,"—specially pointed him out as the most worthy of Christian Knights to fill this eminent station. He who with such noble philanthropy founded and presided over the Society of Knights Liberators of the White Slaves in Africa, cannot but shed additional lustre on the Soldiery of the Temple, whose professed object originally was, and yet is, the protection of defenceless pilgrims, and the rescuing of Christians from Infidel bondage. Under such a Chief the Order must prosper, and there are now Colleges or Establishments in England and in many of the principal Cities of Europe.

Thus the very ancient and sovereign Order of the Temple is in full and chivalric existence, like those Orders of Knighthood which were either formed in imitation of it, or had their origin in the same noble principles of chivalry. It has mourned as well as flourished, but there is in its nature and constitution a principle of vitality which has carried it through all the storms of fate; its continuance, by representatives as well as by title, is as indisputable a fact as the existence of any other chivalric fraternity. The Templars of these days claim no titular rank, yet their station is so far identified with that of the other Orders of Knighthood, that they assert equal purity of descent from the same bright source of chivalry; nor is it possible to impugn the legitimate claims to honourable estimation, which the modern brethren of the Temple derive from the antiquity and pristine lustre of their Order, without at the same time shaking to its centre the whole venerable fabric of knightly honour.

ADMIRAL SIR SIDNEY SMITH. Engraved by W. Greatbatch from a picture by F. Opie R.A.

After this short account of the continuation of the Order, which we have extracted from Mill's Chivalry, it may be interesting to describe the present nature and objects of the Institution; and we shall accordingly make a brief abstract of the statutes established by the Convent-General held at Versailles in 1705, under the Grand Mastership of the Regent Duke of Orleans, and by succeeding General Convocations, so far as they relate to these subjects. The Order of the Fellow Soldiers of the Temple consists of two distinct classes, termed a Superior and Inferior Militia; the former comprising all Knights consecrated according to rites, rules, and usages, with their Esquires; and the latter, the humbler brethren or persons admitted *propter artem*, and the candidates, or as they are designated, the *postulants* for the honours of Chivalry. Except as a serving brother,[3] no one is eligible even to the lower grade, who is not of distinguished rank in society, which in Great Britain is understood to imply that station in life which would entitle a gentleman to attend the Court of his Sovereign. The Candidate must moreover be strongly recommended by Sponsors as a Christian of liberal education, eminent for virtue, morals, and good breeding, and in no case is a scrutiny into these qualifications dispensed with, unless the aspirant be a Knight of Christ, a Teutonic Knight, or the descendant of a Knight Templar. Should he be ambitious of the rank of Novice Esquire, which usually precedes Knighthood, he is farther called on to produce proofs of nobility in the fourth generation; and a deficiency in this requisite can only be supplied by a formal decree of the Grand Master, conferring on him the nobility necessary for his reception. Considerable fees are paid by all entrants; and members, on being promoted to the equestrian honours of the Order, are expected to make an oblation to the Treasury, the amount of which cannot be less than four drams of gold,[4] but generally very far exceeds that sum. Before receiving the vow of profession, which is still administered to all Chevaliers,[5] the Candidate makes a solemn declaration either that he does not belong to the Order of Malta,[6] or that he abjures the spirit of rival hostility which actuated the Knights of St. John in former days against the Templars. These preliminaries being arranged, his petition is finally decided on, either in a Conventual house, or by the special legate of the Grand Master, in whose name only his reception can be proclaimed, and once armed a Knight, and consecrated a Chevalier of the Temple, he cannot on any pretence whatever renounce the Order.[7]

At the head of the Hierarchy of the Order, ranks the Convent-General, or assembly of the Knights, but the executive power is vested in the Grand Master, whose authority is almost unbounded. He is elected for life from among the Knights, and it is declared impious to substitute a successor to him unless he be deceased, or shall have voluntarily abdicated; he may even nominate his successor by testament or otherwise to the Convent-General. He can create new houses and dignities on the Order, cancelling those already constituted, remit penalties, and confer all benefices and offices, the collation to which is not specially provided for in the statutes. He confirms all Diplomas of profession and patents of appointment, and may send legates possessing powers delegated by himself to different countries. His interpretation of the laws is valid, even against a statute of the Convent-General, and he alone has the power of proposing alterations in the rules to that assembly.

Next in honour to the Grand Master, unless he has publicly appointed a delegate or successor, are his four Deputes, or *Vicarii Magistrales*, who are nominated by himself, and removable at his pleasure. After these follow the Members of the Grand Council, which consists of the Supreme Preceptor, and eight Grand Preceptors, the Primate of the Order, and his four Coadjutors General, with all the Grand Priors, Ministers, and other principal dignitaries that may be present at the Magisterial City. Each nation of the Order is presided over by its Grand Prior, appointed for life, whose language comprises the various subordinate divisions of Bailiwicks or Provinces; Commanderies; Convents of Knights and Noviciate Esquires; Abbeys of Ladies and Canonesses; Chapters of Postulants, and Conclaves of Initiation. Except in special cases, no Chevalier is eligible for a Commandery before the expiration of two years from his having obtained the honours of knighthood, and in like manner no Commander can be appointed a Bailli, nor any Bailli a Grand Prior, before the same period has intervened.

In order that the objects of the Institution may be distinctly understood, we shall now proceed to translate a decree by the present Grand Master, bearing date the 4th September 1826, in explanation of the Vow of Profession which has been already referred to, observing, at the same time, that the Order of the Temple, being exclusively devoted to the Christian religion, cannot be considered in the slightest degree connected with Free Masonry, which, it is well known, welcomes equally to its bosom the Jew and the Gentile, the Christian and the Mahommedan, requiring from each only a belief in a Divine Being, with a just sense of moral rectitude and conscientious obligation.

The decree alluded to states, that as the Vow contains many *dispositions* which, misconstructed, might appear incompatible with the advance of knowledge and manners of the age, it is declared that Candidates sign it under the following interpretation:—

1st, That by the Vow of Poverty, the Order does not mean to submit the Chevaliers to an absolute poverty, but to remind them that they ought always to be ready to share their fortune with the unfortunate, and to sacrifice it for the wants of the Order.

2d, That the vow of chastity, and of abhorring lewdness, is the solemn engagement of fulfilling the obligation that society imposes on all men to labour to overcome their vicious propensities, in order not to outrage either decency or morality.

3d, That the obedience due to the Grand Master, and to the dignitaries of the Order, does not exclude the duty imposed on every chevalier of conforming himself, as a man, to natural right, and of obeying, as a citizen, the government of his country.

4th, Lastly, That the Templars are not actuated by the desire of material conquests,—that their principal aim is not to recover the dominions of which the Order was despoiled, or the earth which received the body of Jesus the Christ, but to reconquer to the doctrine for which was precipitated into the tomb that divine preceptor of men,—the empire which it always had over the people when it was revealed to them in all its purity,—in a word, that the Templars are not ambitious of subduing the physical universe to their domination, but the nations that cover it to Christian morality.

It has frequently been asserted, that the Templars have always professed a religion peculiar to themselves, and much at variance with almost every religious creed at present in existence, but on this subject it is only necessary to say here, that although they possess many religious documents of an extraordinary nature, and, amongst others, a very ancient Greek manuscript of *Evangile* and the Epistle of St. John, differing from the version contained in the vulgate, yet no chevalier is obliged to subscribe to them unless he be a candidate for certain offices in the Order. This subject is fully explained in a work lately published at Paris, "Recherches Historiques sur les Templiers et sur leurs Croyances Religieuses par J. Plivard, officier superieur d'Artillerie;" and, for the present, we are unwilling to enter upon it, not having as yet received the *proces verbal* of the Convent-General of the Order, lately assembled at Paris, to which the following question, under the authority of the Grand Master, was submitted:—"L'ordre etant Cosmopolite, et d'après le veu de profession dans la Chevalerie, est il convenable de laisser subsister dans les statuts des dispositions par lesquelles certains officiers de l'Ordre ne pouvent être choisis que parmis les Chevaliers professant la religion Johannite?"

The habit of the Order[8] consists, as formerly, of the white tunic and mantle, with the red cross on the left breast; a white cap with a red feather; a white silk sash fringed with red; white pantaloons, buff-boots, gold spurs and an equestrian sword with a silver hilt. The dress differs somewhat according to the rank of the individual, but every Chevalier is bound to wear the gold ring of profession, with the Cross of the Order, and the letters, P. D. E. P.[9] together with his own name, and the date of his reception engraven thereon. Each Knight also is decorated with the conventual cross or jewel of the Order, which consists of a gold cross of eight points enamelled white, surmounted by the Grand Master's crown, and bearing on its centre a cross pattee enamelled gules.

In concluding these observations, we regret to say that the Order of the Temple, notwithstanding its undeniable claims to honourable distinction, has never enjoyed much consideration amongst our countrymen. Its exclusive character, together with the great expense and difficulty which attend admission into its ranks, no Englishman being legitimately eligible, unless formally recommended by the illustrious Grand Prior of England, has raised against it a host of enemies. Hence, calumnies have been propagated against it, and an institution perfectly unconnected with politics, and actuated by the purest principles of Christian Philanthropy, [10] has been represented as engendering false notions of Government and wild infidelity. But the registers of the Temple contain the respected names of Massillon and Fenelon; Frederick the Great, and Napoleon[11] sanctioned its ceremonies, and honoured its officers; and even in these days, princes of the blood, and some of the most illustrious nobles, of our own and other countries, have not disdained to display the humble ring of profession, along with the gorgeous decorations of the Garter and the Golden Fleece. Scattered over the mighty empire of Great Britain, there are not more than forty subjects of Her Majesty who are Knights Templars; and the whole Members of the Order do not probably at this moment exceed three hundred; but we assert, without fear of contradiction, that no institution equally limited can boast of a greater number of distinguished and honourable associates.

---

1. A copy of this remarkable Charter, the original of which I had an opportunity of examining through the kindness of the Grand Master and Sir Sidney Smith, at Paris, will be found in the Appendix. The Charter was submitted to the inspection of nearly 200 Knights of the Order, at the Convent-General held at Paris in 1810.
2. The following anecdote of Sir Sidney Smith may not be inappropriate here, as relating to a Soldier of the Cross:—

    After the signal defeat of Buonaparte at Acre, the tyrant Djezzar, to avenge himself upon the Franks, inflicted severe punishment on the Jewish and Christian inhabitants of Saphet, and, it is said, had resolved to massacre all the believers in Moses and Jesus Christ, who might be found within his dominions. But Sir Sidney Smith, on being apprized of his intention, instantly caused the Turk to be informed, that if a single Christian head should fall, he would bombard Acre, and burn it about his ears. This decisive interposition of the gallant Admiral is still remembered in the hearts of the inhabitants.

    Such was the confidence placed by them in their deliverer, that Burckhardt, alluding to Sir Sidney, says,—"His word, I have often heard both Turks and Christians exclaim, was like

God's word—it never failed;" and Professor Loĕwe, recently returned from Palestine, affirmed, that the Firmaun of Sir Sidney at once procured for him, both from the Sultan and the Pacha of Egypt, every assistance and facility in pursuing his learned hieroglyphical and mythological researches.

In connection with our subject, it may be mentioned as a singular fact, that Sir Sidney Smith was the first Christian ever permitted to enter the Holy City of Jerusalem armed, since the days of the Crusaders, which he was allowed to do as a special compliment, after the surrender of the French army in Egypt. By his means, also, his followers were granted the like privilege.

Several official documents, relating to Sir Sidney as a Knight Templar, are inserted in the Appendix.

3. The exact condition, or relative position, of the serving Brothers in ancient times is not very perfectly known. That they sometimes held a responsible, and even high command, is proved by the following passage from Michaud's "Bibliographie des Croisades," referring to the work of an old Latin annalist,—"A la page 540 se trouve une lettre d'un *Chevalier Servant* (Dapiferi) de la milice du Temple, addressée au Grand Maître Eberard des Barres, qui était revenu en France avec le roi Louis VII. Dans cette lettre sont peints les malheurs de la Terre Sainte après la morte du prince d'Antioche. Le Chevalier Servant prie le Grand Maître de revenir promptement porter du secours au Chrétiens, réduit à l'extremité. Cette Lettre est de 1149 ou 1150." A serving Brother here appears acting the part of chief officer in the East.

4. Equal to about 50 Francs.

5. For the Vow, vide Appendix.

6. The Order of the Hospitallers of Malta, although in these days almost unheard of, still exists through its members, scattered over Europe. Few, if any, of the old Knights who belonged to the Order in its palmy days are now alive. One of the last of these was the Chevalier Grĕche, who died at Malta in 1838, where he had continued to linger amid the scenes of his Order's former greatness and glory. He was of a French family, and, it is said, spoke French of the time of Louis XIV. He was page to the last Grand Master at Malta, in which capacity there is a full-length portrait of him in the palace of a Portuguese Knight. He often used to look at this picture; pointing the while to his wrinkles and white hair, and laughing at the change from the fair face and flowing locks represented in the painting. Until he became very infirm, he was fond of society, and was frequently

to be met with at the houses of the English, by whom he was much esteemed on account of his interesting recollections and traditions. It is believed that there now remains only one member of the Order as it existed before the dispersion, and he belongs to the *Langue d'Italie*. The Vow of the Knights of St John will be found in the Appendix.

7. We give the following extracts from the statutes themselves:— Art. 308—Nullus ad novitiatum armigerorum accedit, nisi genere in quarto gradu sit nobilis. Art. 310.—Si quis, virtute præstantissimus, novitiatum armigerorum postulans, non sit nobili natus genere, audita Conventus relatione petitoria, a Commendariæ, Ballivatus et Linguæ congressibus, sicut et a Comitiis Statutariis Curiaque Præceptoriali, sancita, illum ordini nobilium, in quarto gradu, adscribendi potestatem solus habet in Militia Templi Supremus Magister. Art. 315.— Quacumque de causa, ab Ordine deficere Equiti nefas est. Si autem honoribus Equestribus vel Militia indignus, judicatus fuerit Eques, in proprii Conventus albo, singulisque Conventuum, Abbatiarum, Postulantiarum initiationisque Cœtuum albis, pro sententia, adnotatur: Vel ab Equestribus Honoribus suspensus: vel, ab Equestri Militia interdictus: vel Utraque Militia indignus. Art. 390.—Nullus ad initiationem accedit, nisi Christianus, liberaliter institutus, civili ordine insignis, virtute, moribus, fide et urbanitate præstantissimus. Art. 391.—In militia inferiori aggregari possunt minoris conditionis viri qui, propter artem, Ordini perutiles esse possunt. Art. 392.—Ad quemcumque Ordinis gradum quemlibet cooptare potest Supremum Magister. Cooptatus autem frater vel in Conventu, vel in Capitulo, vel in Cœtu, sicut et in Abbatiâ cooptata soror, juxta Magistrale Decretum, recipitur, solemniumque rituum et usuum in receptione solitorum immunis fieri, potest, Equestri Consecratione excepta, qua nullus donatur nisi votis solemnibus susceptis. Art. 408.—Templi Commilitonum Posteri; Equites Christi; Equites Teutonici; Patres a mercede; Patres a redemptione captivorum, si jubeat Lingualis Congressus, in inferioribus domibus admittuntur, sicut et ad Novitiatum armigerorem illico provehuntur, tenenturque tantum fide dare jusjurandum

    Statuta Commilitonum Ordinis Templi e regulis sancitis in Conventibus Generalibus prosertim in Conventu Generali Versaliano, Anno Ordinis 586, et in Conventibus Generalibus Lutetianis, A. O. 693, et 695, confecta et in unum codicem coacta.

8. We shall be excused referring to this subject, considering that it engaged so much of the attention of the pious St. Bernard. Respecting the habit of the early Templars, he says, chap, xxii and xxv, "It is granted unto none to wear white tunics or mantles, but to the Knights of Christ.—If any brother wish to have the handsomest or best mantle, either as of due or out of pride, for such presumption, he will, without doubt, deserve the very worst."

9. Pro Deo et Patria. This is one of the present mottoes of the Order. The other, Ferro non auro se muniunt, is taken from the following striking expressions of St. Bernard,—"Equites Christi intus fide, foras ferro non auro se muniunt, non turbulenti aut impetuosi, et quasi ex levitate præcipites, sed consulte atque cum omni cautela et providentia se ipsos ordinentes, et disponentes in aciem, juxta quod de patribus scriptum est. Ita denique vero, quodam ac singulare modo, cernuntur et agnis mitiores et leonibus ferociores:"—Ex. Lib. Sanct. Bernard, Abbat Milit. Templ. cap. 4, No. 8.

10. La société des Templiers vient d'en offrir une preuve éclatante, à l'occasion du mariage de S. M. l'Empereur et Roi avec Marie Louise, d'Autriche. Le 16 Août 1810, elle a donné une fête, terminée par une distribution de vêtemens, des vivres et d'argent à des vieillards indigens choisis dans les douze municipalités des Paris. On peut voir dans le proces verbal qu'ils en out fait imprimer les témoignages flatteurs d'estime qu'ils ont reçu de M. M. les Maires des arrondissemens de Paris et des membres de plusieurs bureaux de bienfaisance.—Thory.

11. En 1811, Napoleon, empereur, revenant a ses idées sur l'importance de cet ordre, tant sous le rapport civil que sous le rapport religieux, fit appeler le grand-maitre Bernard-Raymond, et après plusieurs questions a sa maniere sur l'êtat actuel de l'ordre, sur ses statuts, etc. il s'informa des époques de ses assemblées. Apprenant qu'il y en aurait bientôt une pour la célébration de l'anniversaire du martyre de Jacques de Molay, l'empereur s'empara de cette circonstance, et donna des ordres pour que cette ceremonie se fit publiquement avec une grand pompe religieuse et militaire. Une place d'honneur était réservée pour le grand-maitre et ses lieutenans generaux. M. Clouet, chanoine de Notre-Dame, coadjuteur-general du primat du Temple, et revêtu du camail primatial, prononça l'oraison funèbre du grand-maitre martyr, dont le catafalque était richement orné des insignes de la souveraineté magistrale et patriarcale. On peut se souvenir de l'étonnement que pro-

duisit cette grande ceremonie par sa publicité, ainsi que des conjectures auxquelles elle donna lieu; tout porte à croire que l'empereur se proposait de tirer bon parti de l'ordre du Temple et de son culte s'il ne pouvait parvenir a maîtriser a cour de Rome.

L'empereur don Pedro, après avoir accepté le titre de premier chevalier d'honneur du Temple, autorisa un de ses ministres a recevoir le brevet de grand-prieur titulaire du Bresil; et l'on ne peut douter, d'après la correspondance de ce ministre avec le grand-maitre Bernard-Raymond, que don Pedro n'eut l'intention de faire refleurir l'ordre du Temple au Bresil, comme aussi il avait été sauvé de sa destruction en 1312 par le roi Denis, qui créa l'ordre des chevaliers proscrits par le décret de Clement V.—

Biographie des Hommes du Jour. *Paris, 1836.*

CHAP. V. THE KNIGHTS TEMPLARS OF SCOTLAND.

The Knights of the Temple were introduced into Scotland before 1153 by King David the First, who established them at Temple on the Southesk,[1] and who was so attached to the brotherhood, that we are told by an old historian "Sanctus David de prœclara Militia Templi optimos fratres secum retinens, eos diebus et noctibus morum suorum fecit esse custodes."[2] Malcolm, the grandson of David, conferred on the brethren "in liberam et puram Elymosynam unum plenarium Toftum in quolibet Burgo totius terræ," which foundation was enlarged by his successors, William the Lion and Alexander the Second. The charter of the latter is still in the possession of Lord Torphichen, whereby he grants and confirms "Deo et fratribus Templi Salomonis de Jerusalem omnes illas rectitudines, libertatis et consuetudines quas Rex David et Rex Malcolm et decessus pater meus Rex Willielmus eis dederunt et concesserunt, sicut scripta eorum authentica attestant." This curious document, after enumerating certain of these rights and liberties, scilicet,— the king's sure peace; the privilege of buying, selling, and trading with all his subjects; freedom from all tribute and toll, &c. proceeds "Et nullus eis injuriam faciat, vel fieri consentiat super meam defensionem, Et ubicunque in tota terra mea ad judiorum (*q. judicium*) venerint, causa eorum primum tractata, et prius rectum suum habeant, et postea faciant. Et nullus ponat hominem predictorum fratrum nostrorum ad foram judicii si noluerint, &c. Et omnes libertates et consuetudines quas ipsi per alias regiones habent in terra mea ubique habeant."

These general privileges, throughout Europe, were very extensive. The Templars were freed from all tythes to the church, and their priests were entitled to celebrate mass, and to absolve from sins to the same extent as bishops, a privilege which was strongly objected to by the latter. Their houses possessed the right of sanctuary or asylum for criminals. They could be witnesses in their own cause, and were exempted from giving testimony in the cause of others. They were relieved by the papal bulls from all taxes, and from subjection and obedience to any secular power. By these great immunities, the Order was rendered in a manner independent, but it would appear, nevertheless, that both the Templars and Hospitallers considered themselves subjects of the countries to which they belonged, and took part in the national wars, for we find by the Ragman Roll, "Freere Johan de Sautre, Mestre de la Chevalier del Temple en Ecoce," and another Brother, swearing fealty to Edward I. in 1296; and the author of the Annals of Scotland, taking notice of the Battle of Falkirk, 12th July 1298, informs us, that the only persons of note who fell were Brian le Jay, Master of the English Templars, and the Prior of Torphichen in Scotland, a Knight of another Order of religious soldiery. The former of these Chevaliers met his death by the hand of the redoubted Sir William Wallace, who advanced alone from the midst of his little band, and slew him with a single blow, although the historian adds, that Sir Brian le Jay was a Knight Templar of high military renown, who had shewn himself most active against the Scots.[3]

Little is known of the farther History of the Knights Templars in Scotland from the time of Alexander II. down to the beginning of the 14th century, excepting that their privileges were continued to them by succeeding Kings, whose bounty and piety were in those ages continually directed towards the religious Orders. By their endowments, and the bequests of the nobles, the possessions of the Order came to be so extensive, that their lands were scattered "per totum regnum Scotiæ, a limitibus versus Angliam, et sic discendo per totum regnum usque ad

Orchades." Besides the House of the Temple in Mid-Lothian, the following Establishments or Priories of the Order may be enumerated, viz. St. Germains, in East Lothian; Inchynan, in Renfrewshire; Maryculter, in Kincardineshire; Aggerstone, in Stirlingshire; Aboyne, in Aberdeenshire; Derville or Derval, in Ayr-shire; Dinwoodie, in Dumfriesshire; Red-abbey-stedd, in Roxburghshire, and Temple Liston, in West-Lothian.

The date of the spoliation of the Templars of Scot-land, corresponds of course with that of the persecu-tion of the Order in other countries, and it is to the credit of our forefathers that we can obtain no ac-count of any Member of the Brotherhood having been subjected to personal torture or suffering amongst them; their estates, however, appear to have been duly transferred to the possession of their rivals, the Knights Hospitallers; into which Order it is not im-probable that, like their Brethren in England, a number of the Templars entered.

In November 1309, John de Soleure, the Papal Legate, and William, Bishop of St. Andrews, held an Inquisitorial Court at the Abbey of Holyrood to in-vestigate the charges against the Templars, but Walter de Clifton, Grand Preceptor of the Order in North Britain,[4] and William de Middleton, were the only two Knights who appeared before the Tribunal, the proceedings of which, as recorded at length in Wilkins' Consilia, make no allusion to any punish-ment being inflicted, so that we may fairly conclude they were soon set at liberty. The Preceptor, in his examination, readily confessed that the rest of the Brethren had fled, and dispersed themselves *propter scandalium exortum contra ordinem*, and we are told by a learned French writer, that having deserted the Temple, they had ranged themselves under the banners of Robert Bruce, by whom they were formed into a new Order, the observances of which were based on those of the Templars, and became, according to him, the source of Scottish Free Masonry.[5] This statement corresponds with the celebrated Charter of Larmenius already referred to, in which the Scottish Templars are excommunicated as *Templi desertores, anathemate percussos*; and along with the Knights of St. John, *dominiorum Militiæ spoliatores*, placed for ever beyond the pale of the Temple, *extra gyrum Templi nunc, et in futurum*; and it is likewise supported in some measure by the authority of the accurate historian of Free Masonry, M. Thory, who, in his "Acta Latomorum," states that Robert Bruce founded the Masonic Order of Heredom de Kilwinning, after the Battle of Bannockburn, reserving to himself and his successors on the Throne of Scotland, the office and title of Grand Master. Scottish tradition has, moreover, always been in favour of this origin of the Ancient Mother Kilwinning Lodge, which certainly at one time possessed other degrees of Masonry besides those of St. John; and it is well known to our Masonic readers, that there are even in our own days at Edinburgh, a few individuals claiming to be the representatives of the Royal Order established by Bruce, which, though now nearly extinct in this country,[6] still flourishes in France, where it was established by Charter from Scotland, and even by the Pretender himself, in the course of last century, and is now conferred as the highest and most distinguished grade of Masonry, sanctioned by the Grand Orient, under the title of the *Rose Croix de Heredom de Kilwinning*. It may be interesting to add, that the introduction on the Continent of this ancient branch of our national Masonry, has been commemorated by a splendid medal struck at Paris, bearing, amongst other devices, the Royal Arms and Motto of Scotland; and that the Brethren of the Lodge of Constancy at Arras, still preserve with reverence an original charter of the Order, granted to their Chapter in 1747, by Charles Edward Stuart, and signed by that unfortunate Prince himself as the representative of the Scottish Kings.[7] Nor can any thing indicate more strongly the high estimation in which the chivalry of the Rosy Cross of Kilwinning is held in France, than the fact that the Prince Cambaceres, Arch-chancellor of the Empire, presided over it as Provincial Grand Master, (the office of supreme head being inherent in the Crown of Scotland,) for many years; and that he was succeeded in his dignity, if we mistake not, by the head of the illustrious family of Choiseul.

But whether the Scottish Templars really joined the victorious standard of Robert Bruce, and with him, as our countrymen would fain hope, fought and conquered at Bannockburn, or whether the majority of them transferred themselves along with the possessions of the Order, to the Knights of St. John of

Jerusalem, certain it is, that from the time of the persecution, the Order of the Temple, together with all its wealth, became merged in that of the Hospitallers, though certainly not to such a degree as to obliterate all distinct traces of the Red Cross Knights. On the contrary, we find by a public document recorded entire in the Register of the Great Seal of Scotland, and dated *two centuries* after the incorporation of the Orders, that King James the Fourth confirmed all former grants *sancto Hospitali de Jerusalem, et fratribus ejusdem militiæ Templi Salomonis*,—a satisfactory proof that the Order, although proscribed by the Pope, was still retained conjointly with that of the Hospital, in law papers at least.[8]

The Knights of St. John had also been introduced into Scotland by King David the First, and had a charter granted to them by Alexander the Second, two years after that to the Templars. The Preceptory of Torphichen, in West Lothian, was their first, and continued to be their chief residence, and by the accession of the Temple lands and other additions, their property at the time of the Reformation came to be immense. When that event took place, the chief dignitary or Grand Preceptor of the Order in Scotland, with a seat as a Peer in Parliament, was Sir James Sandilands, a cadet of the family of Calder, whose head, as is well known to readers of Scottish History, was the private friend of John Knox, and one of the first persons of distinction to embrace the reformed religion. We might suspect, that even before the promulgation of the statute 1560, prohibiting all allegiance within the realm to the See of Rome, the former personage had become indifferent to the charge confided to him by the Order; for a rescript from the Grand Master and Chapter at Malta, dated so early as the 1st of October 1557, and addressed to him, is still on record, wherein they complain "that many of the possessions, jurisdictions, &c. were conveyed or taken away from them contrary to the statutes and oaths, and to the damnation of the souls, as well of those who possessed them, as of those who, without sufficient authority, yielded them up; producing thereby great detriment to religion and the said Commandery;" but be this as it may, we are certain that the conversion of Sir James Sandilands, or as he was termed, the Lord of St. John of Jerusalem in Scotland, was followed by his surrender to the Crown of the whole possessions of the combined Templars and Hospitallers, which having been declared forfeited to the State on the ground that "the principal cause of the foundation of the Preceptory of Torphichen, *Fratribus Hospitalis Hierosolimitani, Militibus Templi Salomonis,* was the service enjoined to the Preceptor on oath to defend and advance the Roman Catholic Religion," were by a process of transformation well understood by the Scottish Parliament of those days, converted into a Temporal Lordship, which the unfortunate Queen Mary, then only twenty years of age, and newly established amongst her Scottish subjects, in consideration of a payment of ten thousand crowns of the Sun, and of his *fidele, nobile, et gratuitum, servitium, nobis nostrisque patri et matri bonæ memoriæ*, conferred on, or rather retransferred to the Ex Grand Preceptor himself and his heirs with the title of Torphichen, which, although the estate is much dilapidated, still remains in his family.[9] All this was transacted acted on the petition of Sir James Sandilands himself, with the formal approbation of the National Legislature; and after renouncing the profession of a soldier-monk, we find that the last of Scottish Preceptors of St. John became married and lived to a good old age, having died so late as 1596 without issue, when the title of Torphichen passed to his grand nephew, the lineal descendant of his elder brother, Sir John Sandilands of Calder.

We shall not pause to consider whether a body of Masonic Templars unconnected with the Hospitallers, and representing the Royal Order which Bruce is said to have instituted from the relict of the Ancient Knights, has been perpetuated in Scotland since the days of Bannockburn, having no means of illustrating so obscure a subject; but, with all due respect to the learned French writer, whose authority we have already quoted, we may observe, that the Masonic Tradition of the country does not connect the Templars with Bruce's Order in any way whatever, but, on the contrary, invariably conjoins those Knights with the Hospitallers, and consequently points to the period of the renunciation of Popery, as the time when they first sought refuge, and a continuance of their Chivalry among the "Brethren of the Mystic Tie." The Chevaliers also of the Rosy Cross of Kilwinning in France, own no alliance with Masonic

Templary, which they consider a comparatively modern invention; nor do there exist, so far as we know, any authentic records anterior to the Reformation, to prove a connection between the Knights Templars and Freemasons in any part of the world, though we must not omit to mention, that a formal document in the Latin language is said to be deposited in a Lodge at Namur on the Meuse, purporting to be a proclamation by the Freemasons of Europe, "of the Venerable Society sacred to John," assembled by representatives from London, Edinburgh, Vienna, Amsterdam, Paris, Madrid, Venice, Brussels, and almost every other Capital City, at Cologne on the Rhine in 1535; and signed, amongst others, by the famous Melancthon, in which, after declaring that "to be more effectually vilified and devoted to public execration, they had been accused of reviving the Order of the Templars," they solemnly affirm, that "the Freemasons of St. John derive not their origin from the Templars, nor from any other Order of Knights; neither have they any, or the least communication with them directly, or through any manner of intermediate tie, being far more ancient," &c.—all of which would imply, that some sort of connection was understood in those days to exist between certain of the Masonic Fraternities and the Knights Templars. A Copy of this document was sent to Edinburgh in 1826, by M. de Marchot, an Advocate at Nivelles, and a translation of it has been inserted under the attestation of a Notary Public in the Records of the Ancient Lodge of Edinburgh, (Mary's Chapel); but we have little faith in German documents on Free Masonry, unless supported by other testimony; and as no Historian of the Craft makes the slightest allusion to the great Convocation of the Brethren at Cologne, in the sixteenth century, rather than ask the reader to believe that it ever took place, we shall presume that M. de Marchot may have been deceived.[10]

From the era of the Reformation, the combined Order appears in Scotland only as a Masonic body; but there are some records to indicate that, so early as 1590, a few of the brethren had become mingled with the Architectural Fraternities, and that a Lodge at Stirling, patronised by King James, had a Chapter of Templars attached to it, who were termed cross-legged Masons; and whose initiatory ceremonies were performed not in a room, but in the Old Abbey, the ruins of which are still to be seen in the neighbourhood. The next authentic notice we can find on this subject, is in M. Thory's excellent Chronology of Masonry, wherein it is recorded, that about 1728, Sir John Mitchell Ramsay, the well-known author of Cyrus, appeared in London, with a system of Scottish Masonry, up to that date, perfectly unknown in the metropolis, tracing its origin from the Crusades, and consisting of three degrees, the *Ecossais*, the *Novice*, and the *Knight Templar*. The English Grand Lodge rejected the system of Ramsay, who, as is well known, along with the other adherents of the Stuart Family, transferred it to the Continent, where it became the corner-stone of the *hauts grades*, and the foundation of those innumerable ramifications into which an excellent and naturally simple institution has been very uselessly extended in France, Germany, and other countries abroad.[11]

In pursuing the very curious subject of the *hauts grades,* we may observe, however, that they never obtained much consideration during the lifetime of Ramsay, although they are invariably traced to him and to Scotland, the fairy land of Foreign Masonry,[12] but gathered their chief impulse from the disgraceful dissentions in the Masonic Lodges at Paris, about the middle of last century, which induced the Chevalier de Bonneville, and other distinguished persons at the Court of France, to form themselves into a separate institution, named the Chapitre de Clermont, in honour of one of the Princes of the Blood, Louis de Bourbon, Prince de Clermont, then presiding over the Masonic Fraternities. In this Chapter they established, amongst other degrees, Ramsay's system of the Masonic Templars, which, along with other high grades, was soon conveyed into the Northern Kingdoms of Europe, by the Officers of the French Army, but especially, by the Marquis de Bernez, and the Baron de Hund, the latter of whom made it the ground-work of his Templar *Regime de la Stricte Observance,* which occupied, for several years, so prominent a place in the Secret Societies of Germany. This adventurer appeared in that country with a patent, under the sign-manual of Prince Charles Edward Stuart, appointing him Grand Master of the seventh province; but although he had invented a plausible tale in support of his title and authority,—both of

which he affirmed had been made over to him by the
Earl Marischal on his death-bed,—and of the antiquity of his order, which he derived, of course, from
Scotland, where the chief seat of the Templars was
Aberdeen, [13] —the imposture was soon detected, and
it was even discovered that he had himself enticed
and initiated the ill-fated Pretender into his fabulous
order of Chivalry. The delusions on this subject, however, had taken such a hold in Germany, that they
were not altogether dispelled, until a deputation had
actually visited Aberdeen, and found amongst the
worthy and astonished brethren there, no trace either
of very ancient Templars or Freemasonry. [14] From
some of the Continental States, it is conjectured that
Masonic Templary was transplanted into England
and Ireland, in both of which countries it has continued to draw a languid existence, unconnected with
any remnant of the Knights of St. John, whose incorporation in the Scottish Order, is one of the most remarkable features of that Institution. We are happy to
add, nevertheless, that the most fraternal feelings and
intercourse subsist between the Scottish brethren and
the Templars of the sister kingdoms, and we can our-
selves testify to the cordiality with which the former
are received in the encampments of London.

During the whole of the eighteenth century the
combined Order of the Temple and Hospital in Scotland can be but faintly traced, though I have the as-
surance of well-informed Masons that thirty or forty
years ago they knew old men who had been members of it for sixty years, and it had sunk so low at the

time of the French Revolution, that the sentence which the Grand Lodge of Scotland fulminated in 1792 against all degrees of Masonry except those of St. John, was expected to put a period to its existence. Soon after this, however, some active individuals revived it, and with the view of obtaining documentary authority for their chapters, as well as of avoiding any infringement of the statutes then recently enacted against secret societies, adopted the precaution of accepting charters of constitution from a body of Masonic Templars, named the Early Grand Encampment, in Dublin, of whose origin we can find no account, and whose legitimacy, to say the least, was quite as questionable as their own. Several charters of this description were granted to different Lodges of Templars in Scotland about the beginning of the present century, but these bodies maintained little concert or intercourse with each other, and were certainly not much esteemed in the country. Affairs were in this state when, about 1808, Mr. Alexander Deuchar was elected Commander, or Chief of the Edinburgh Encampment of Templars, and his brother, Major David Deuchar, along with other Officers of the Royal Regiment, was initiated into the Order. This infusion of persons of higher station and better information gave an immediate impulse to the Institution, and a General Convocation of all the Templars of Scotland, by representatives, having taken place at the Capital, they unanimously resolved to discard the Irish Charters, and to rest their claims, as the representatives of the Knights of old, on the general belief of the country in their favour, and the well-accredited traditions handed down from their forefathers. They further determined to entreat the Duke of Kent, who was a Chevalier du Temple, as well as the chief of the Masonic Templars in England, to become the Patron Protector of the Order in North Britain, offering to submit themselves to His Royal Highness in that capacity, and to accept from him a formal Charter of Constitution, erecting them into a regular Conclave of Knights Templars, and Knights of St. John of Jerusalem. The Duke of Kent lost no time in complying with their request, and his Charter bears date 19th of June 1811. By a provision in it, Mr. Deuchar, who had been nominated by the Brethren, was appointed Grand Master for life.

These wise and vigorous measures rescued the Order from obscurity; and in its improved condition, we find that it continued rapidly to flourish, numbering, in the course of a few years, no less than forty encampments or lodges in different parts of the British dominions holding of its Conclave. In 1828, the Order seemed to have received a fresh impulse, and assumed a novel and interesting aspect by the judicious introduction of the ancient chivalric costume and forms. Dissentions, however, unfortunately occurred, from 1830 to 1835, tending to impede the further progress of the Order; and for a while it may be said to have again almost fallen into abeyance. In the end of the latter year, a committee of ten gentlemen was appointed to settle all differences, as well as to frame proper regulations for the future government of the

Order. Under their arrangement and arbitration, the present statutes were established, and a reconciliation effected between the contending parties. In January 1836, Admiral Sir David Milne, K. C. B. was unanimously elected Grand Master, and at a general election in the same month, Lord Ramsay (now Earl of Dalhousie) was appointed his Depute, the various other offices in the Order being filled by gentlemen, generally well known, and of a respectable station in society. In the course of three months after the re-union, not fewer than a hundred persons, chiefly men of fortune, officers, and members of the learned professions, had been received into the Order in the Edinburgh Canongate Kilwinning Priory or Encampment alone. Since then, other Priories have been established in the country, and the Institution has assumed an importance and dignity worthy of the highest class of gentlemen connected with the Masonic Institutions of Scotland.

---

1. The original name of Temple on the Southesk, according to Chalmers, was Balantrodach. In the Chartular of Aberdeen the Preceptory is styled "domus Templi de Balantradock;" and in the Chartular of the Abbey of Newbattle we find mentioned, "Magister et Fratres Templi de Blentodoch," which is a contraction or corruption of the same term. The place became known by the designation of Temple only after the establishment of the Order there. This was the head-quarters of the Grand Preceptors of Scotland, and became, at the suppression of the Templars, attached to the Hospital of St. John. In the 15th century, Sir William Knolls, Grand Preceptor of St. John's, obtained an Act of Parliament, changing the old name into that of the barony of St. John. But the people never conformed to the alteration. Part of the foundations of the original convent were dug

up about a century ago. The ancient chapel of the Temple continued till lately to be used as the parish kirk. It is now partly dilapidated, in consequence of a new church being built. On the eastern gable there is an antique inscription, formed with lead run into the letters, which appears to be as follows:—

V Æ S A C

M T H M.

These letters, when extended, may signify, *Vitæ Sacrum Militiæ Templi Hierosolymitani*; or, *Virgini Ædem Sacram Militiæ Templi Hierosolymæ Majister*; supplying *condidit* or *consecravit*. The Virgin Mary, it is well known, was the patroness of the Order. What monstrous mysteries would not the ingenious Von Hammer make these letters the vehicle of revealing! In the second line the learned German could not fail to discover the presence of the *Metis* or *Tau* of the Gnostics, whose doctrines, he insists, the Templars held, as attested by their monumental remains, and by coins or medals imagined to refer to them.

2. Book of Cupar quoted in Father Hay's MS.
3. This gallant Templar,—worthy to have fallen in a holier cause, —is thus strangely vilified, after death, by some miscreant, at the trial of the Templars:—"Brian le Jāy dixit quod Jesus Christus non fuit verus Deus et vérus homo; quod minimus pilus barbæ unius Saraceni fuit majoris valoris quam totum corpus istius qui loquitur. Pauperibus quibusdam eleemosynam a Briane petentibus pro amore Dei et beatæ Mariæ Virginis respondit, 'Que dame, allez vous pendre à votre dame;' et projiciens impetuose unum quadrantem in luto, fecit pauperes musare in eodem et hoc tempore frigidæ hyemis." Such is a sample of the evidence against the Order.
4. It appears by the following extract from Clifton's examination, that the Preceptor of Scotland was a subordinate officer to the Master, or Grand Prior in England. "Interrogatus; quis recepit eum ad dictum ordinem et dedit ei habitum? dixit, quod Frater Willielmus de la More oriundus de Comitatu Ebor. tunc et nunc Magister dicti Ordinis in Anglia et Scotia."
5. "Après la mort de Jacques de Molay, des Templiers Ecossais étant devenus apostats, a l'instigation du roi Robert Bruce, se rangèrent sous les bannières d'un nouvel Ordre institué par ce prince, et dans lequel les réceptions furent basées sur celles de l'Ordre du Temple. C'est là qu'il faut chercher l'origine de la Maçonnerie Ecossaise, et même celle des autres Rites maçoniques.—Du schisme qui s'introduisit en Ecosse naquit un grand nombre de sectes. Presque toutes ont la prétention de

dériver du Temple, et quelques unes celle de se dire l'Ordre lui-même."

Manuel des Chevaliers de L'Ordre du Temple. *Paris, 1825.*

The historian, Raymouard, thus formally excuses himself from speculating on the fate of the disbanded Scottish Knights:—"Que devinrent-ils? Ce n'est pas à moi de soulever le voile mystérieux de ces infortunés: l'histoire publique se tait, mon devoir est de me taire comme elle."—Monuments Historiques.

6. An attempt has been very recently made to revive this Order, by the initiation of a number of new members, chiefly Brethren of the Lodge of St. David, Edinburgh.

7. The medal alluded to was struck at the expense of the Chapitre du Choix at Paris, to celebrate the establishment in France of a Provincial Grand Lodge of Heredom de Kilwinning, by a Charter, dated Edinburgh the 1st of May 1786, constituting Mr. John Mattheus, a distinguished merchant of Rouen, Provincial Chief, with very ample powers, to disseminate the Order. The Chapitre du Choix was itself erected by a charter from Edinburgh in the same year, addressed to Nicholas Chabouille, avocat en parlement, and other brethren. Both these documents bear the signatures of William Charles Little, Deputy Grand Master, William Mason, and William Gibb. At a later date, a Provincial Grand Master was also appointed for Spain, in the person of Mr. James Gordon, a merchant at Xeres de la Frontera, whose commission was signed by Deputy Grand Master Dr. Thomas Hay, and Messrs. Charles Moor and John Brown, as heads of the Royal Order. In 1811, there were no less than twenty-six Chapters of Heredom holding of the Provincial Grand Lodge of the Order in France, including some in Belgium and Italy.

—Histoire de la Fondation du Grand Orient de France.
Paris, 1812.

8. An abstract of this interesting document will be found in the Appendix.

9. The reader will find the Preceptor's motives and proceedings explained in an authentic family document printed from a manuscript copy in the Advocates Library, in a little work named, "Templaria. Edinburgh, 1828." We extract from it the following account of the surrender of the Preceptory:—"He personally compeirit in presence of the Queen's Majesty, the Lord Chancelour, the Earles of Murray, Marischall, and diuers others of her Hiehnes Privy Council, and there, as the only lawful undoubted Titular, and present possessor of the Lordship and Pre-

ceptorie of Torphephen, which was never subject to any Chapter or Conuent whatsomever, except only the Knights of Jerusalem and Temple of Solomon, Genibus flexis et reverentia qua decuit, resigned and ouergave in the hands of our Souerane Lady, his undoubted Superior, ad perpetuam remanentiam, all Right, Property, and Possession, which he had, or any way could pretend to the said Preceptorie, or any part thereof, in all time Coming; to the effect the same might remain perpetually, with her Hyeness and her Successours, as a Part of Property and Patrimony of her Crown for ever. After this resignation in the Queen's Majesty's hands, ad Remanentiam, of this Benefice, be the lawful Titular thereof, her Hyeness, in remembrance of the good service of the said Sir James Sandilands, gave and grantid and dispon'd, in feu-farme, heritably, to the said Sir James, his heirs and assignies, All and Haill, the said Preceptorie and Lordship."

That the payment of the above sum of ten thousand crowns of the Sun subsequently involved Sandilands in serious difficulties and embarrassments, we are instructed by the works referred to, in which it is stated that—"albeit the charter bears present payment of ten thousand crowns, that the money was paid at divers times, partly upon Her Majesty's precepts to her servants, French Paris, Sir Robert Melvin, Sir James Balfour, and Captain Anstruther; and the rest of the sum to Mr. Robert Richardson, treasurer for the time, whereof there is a receipt under the privy seal. That a great part of that money, numbered in gold and silver, was borrowed from Timothy Corneoli, an Italian gentleman of the Preceptor's acquaintance at Genoa, and a banker of the house of————resident in Scotland for the time. That this nobleman being burthened with great debts, for his exoneration and relief, was forced to let in feu-farm his own roumes for a reasonable composition," &c.; and he was afterwards obliged to part with some of the larger baronies of the estate.

10. To satisfy the curious, a copy of the translated document is inserted in the Appendix.

11. Il est certain que l'invention des hauts grades maçonniques a fait le plus grand tort á l'institution, en dènaturant son objet, et en l'affublant de titres pompeux et de cordons qui ne lui appartiennent pas. On conviendra que jamais elle n'eût été proscrite, dans une partie d'Allemagne, si les dissentions occasioneés par la Stricte-Observance, les pretentions de soidisant successeurs des Frères de la Rose-Croix, et surtout l'invention de l'illumi-

natisme qu'on introduisit dans quelques L. n'eussent rendu "l'association suspecté aux gouvernemens."—Acta Latomorum.

12. There have been at least a hundred grades of Continental Masonry denominated "Ecossais."

13. On this subject we shall let the Baron de Hund speak for himself:—Les Frères de la Stricte-Observance se disent les successeurs des Templiers, et leur doctrine consiste a perpétuer l'existence de l'Ordre sous le voile de la Franche Maçonnerie. Voici l'Histoire de l'Institution, selon le Baron de Hund; Dans l'année 1303, deux Chevaliers, nommés Noffodoi et Florian, furent punis pour crimes. Tous deux perdirent leurs commanderies et particulièrement, le dernier, celle de Montfaucon. Ils en demandèrent de nouvelles au Gr.-Maître provincial de Mont-Carmel; et comme il les leur refusa, ils l'assassinèrent dans sa maison de campagne, prés de Milan, et cachèrent son corps dans le jardin, sous des arbrisseaux. Ils se réfugièrent ensuite á Paris, ou ils accusèrent l'Ordre des crimes les plus horribles, ce qui entraina sa perte, et par suite le supplice de J. Molay. Après la catastrophe, le Grand-Maître provincial de l'Auvergne, Pierre d'Aumont, s'enfuit avec deux Commandeurs et cinq Chevaliers. Pour n'être point reconnus, ils se déguisèrent en ouvriers maçons, et se réfugièrent dans une ile Ecossaise, ou ils trouvèrent le Grand-Commandeur Hauptoncourt, Georges de Hasris, et plusieurs autres Frères avec lesquels ils résolurent de continuer l'Ordre. Ils tinrent, le jour de St.-Jean 1313, un Chapitre dans lequel Aumont, premier du nom, fut nommé Grand-Maitre. Pour se soustraire aux persécutions, ils empruntèrent des symboles pris dans l'art de la Maçonnerie, et se dénommèrent Maçons libres.... En 1361, le Grand-Maitre du Temple transporta son siege a Aberdeen, et par suite l'Ordre se répandit, sous le voile de la Fr.-Maçonnerie, en Italie, en Allemagne, en France, en Portugal, en Espagne et ailleurs. Der Signatsterne, etc., p. 178.

14. It is stated in the Freemason's Review, that, according to authentic documents, the Aberdeen Lodge has existed since 1541.

APPENDIX

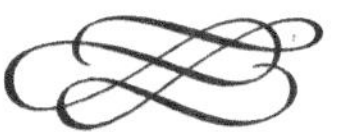

BULL OF POPE CLEMENT V.

Ordinis statum habitum atque nomen, Non Sine Cordis Amaritudine et Dolore sacro approbante concilio, Non Per Modum Definitivæ Sententiæ, cum eam super hoc secundum inquisitiones et processus super his habitos, Non possumus Ferre, de Jure, Sed Per viam Provisionis, seu ordinationis apostolicæ, irrefragabili et Perpetuo Valitura sustulimus sanctione, ipsum prohibitione Perpetuæ supponentes, distinctius inhibendo ne quis dictum Ordinem de cœtero intrare, vel ejus habitum suscipere aut portare, vel pro Templario gerere se præsumeret; quod si quis contra faceret, excommunicationis incurreret sententiam, ipso facto. Datum Viennæ, vi. non. Maii, pont. nostrianno vii. (ii. Maii MCCCIII.)

CHARTER OF TRANSMISSION.

Ego Frater Johannes-Marcus Larmenius, Hierosolymitanus, Dei gratia et Secretissimo Venerandi sanctissimique Martyris, Supremi Templi Militiæ Magistri (cui honos et gloria) decreto, communi Fratrum Consilio confirmato, super universum Templi Ordinem Summo et Supremo Magisterio insignitus, singulis has decretales litteras visuris salutem, salutem, salutem.

Notum sit omnibus tam præsentibus quam futuris, quod, deficientibus, propter extremam ætatem, viribus, rerum angustia et gubernaculi gravitate prepensis, ad majorem Dei gloriam, Ordinis, Fratrum et Statutorum tutelam et salutem ego, supra dictus, humilis Magister Militiæ Templi, inter validiores manus Supremum statuerim deponere Magisterium.

Idcirco, Deo juvante, unoque Supremi Conventus Equitum consensu, apud eminentem Commendatorem et carissimum Fratrem, Franciscum-Thomam-Theobaldum Alexandrinum, Supremum Ordinis Templi Magisterium, auctoritatem et privilegia contuli, et hoc præsenti decreto pro vita confero, cum potestate, secundum temporis et rerum leges, Fratri alteri, institutionis et ingenii nobilitate morumque honestate præstantissimo, Summum et Supremum Ordinis Templi Magisterium summamque auctoritatem conferendi. Quod sic, ad perpetuitatem Magisterii, successorum non intersectam seriem et Statutorum integritatem tuendas. Jubeo tamen ut non transmitti possit Magisterium, sine commilitonum Templi Conventus Generalis consensu, quoties colligi valuerit Supremus iste Conventus; et, rebus ita sese habentibus, successor ad nutum Equitum eligatur.

Ne autem Languescant Supremi Officii munera, sint nunc et perenniter quatuor Supremi Magistri Vicarii, supremam potestatem, eminentiam et auctoritatem, super universum Ordinem, salvo jure Supremi Magistri, habentes; qui Vicarii Magistri apud seniores secundum professionis seriem, eligantur. Quod Statutum e commendato mihi et Fratribus voto sacrosancti supra dicti Venerandi Beatissimique Magistri nostri, Martyris (cui honos et gloria) Amen.

Ego denique, Fratrum Supremi Conventus decreto, e suprema mihi commissa auctoritate, Scotos

Templarios Ordinis desertores, anathemate percussos, illosque et Fratres Sancti Johannis Hierosolymæ, dominiorum Militiæ spoliatores (quibus apud Deum misericordia) extra girum Templi, nunc et in futurum, volo, dico et jubeo.

Signa, ideo, pseudo-Fratribus ignota et ignoscenda constitui, ore commilitonibus tradenda, et quo, in Supremo Conventu, jam tradere modo placuit.

Quæ vero signa tantummodo pateant post debitam professionem et equestrem consecrationem, secundum Templi commilitonum Statuta, ritus et usus, supra dicto eminenti Commendatori a me transmissa, sicut a Venerando et Sanctissimo Martyre Magistro (cui honos et gloria) in meas manus habui tradita. Fiat sicut dixi. Fiat. Amen.

Ego Johannes-Marcus Larmenius dedi, die decima tertia februarii 1324.

Ego Franciscus-Thomas-Theobaldus Alexandrinus, Deo juvante, Supremum Magisterium acceptum habeo, 1324.

Ego Arnulphus De Braque, Deo juvante, Supremum Magisterium acceptum habeo, 1340.

Ego Johannes Claromontanus, Deo juvante, Supremum Magisterium acceptum habeo, 1349.

Ego Bertrandus Duguesclin, Deo juvante, Supremum Magisterium acceptum habeo, 1357.

Ego Johannes Arminiacus, Deo juvante, Supremum Magisterium acceptum habeo, 1381.

Ego Bernardus Arminiacus, Deo juvante, Supremum Magisterium acceptum habeo, 1392.

Ego Johannes Arminiacus, Deo juvante, Supremum Magisterium acceptum habeo, 1419.

Ego Johannes Croyus, Deo juvante, Supremum Magisterium acceptum habeo, 1451.

Ego Robertus Lenoncurtius, Deo juvante, Supremum Magisterium acceptum habeo, 1478.

Ego Galeatius de Salazar, Deo juvante, Supremum Magisterium acceptum habeo, 1497.

Ego Philippus Chabotius, Deo juvante, Supremum Magisterium acceptum habeo, 1516.

Ego Gaspardus De Salciaco, Tavannensis, Deo juvante, Supremum Magisterium acceptum habeo, 1544.

Ego Henricus De Monte Morenciaco, Deo juvante, Supremum Magisterium acceptum habeo, 1574.

Ego Carolus Valesius, Deo juvante, Supremum Magisterium acceptum habeo, 1615.

Ego Jacobus Ruxellius de Grancio, Deo juvante, Supremum Magisterium acceptum habeo, 1651.

Ego Jacobus-Henricus De Duro Forti, dux de Duras, Deo juvante, Supremum Magisterium acceptum habeo, 1681.

Ego Philippus, dux Aurelianensis, Deo juvante, Supremum Magisterium acceptum habeo, 1705.

Ego Ludovicus-Augustus Borbonius, dux du Maine, Deo juvante, Supremum Magisterium acceptum habeo, 1724.

Ego Ludovicus-Henricus Borbonius-Condœus, Deo juvante, Supremum Magisterium acceptum habeo, 1737.

Ego Ludovicus-Franciscus Borbonius-Conty, Deo

juvante, Supremum Magisterium acceptum habeo, 1741.

Ego Ludovicus-Hercules-Timoleo de Cosse-Brissac, Deo juvante, Supremum Magisterium acceptum habeo, 1776.

Ego Claudius-Mathæus Radix de Chevillon, Templi senior Vicarius Magistri, adstantibus Fratribus Prospero-Maria-Petro-Michaele Charpentier de Saintot, Bernardo-Raymundo Fabre-Palaprat, Templi Vicariis Magistris, et Johnne-Baptista-Augusto de Courchant, Supremo Præceptore, hasce litteras decretales a Ludovico-Hercule-Timoleone de Cosse-Brissac, supremo Magistro, in temporibus infaustis mihi depositas, Fratri Jacobo-Philippo Ledru, Templi seniori Vicario Magistro tradidi, ut istæ litteræ, in tempore opportuno, ad perpetuam Ordinis nostri memoriam, juxta ritum (voyez le Rituel levitique) Orientalem, vigeant: Die decima junii 1804.

Ego Bernardus-Raymundus Fabre-Palaprat, Deo juvante, Supremum Magisterium acceptum habeo: Die quarta novembris 1804.

VOW OF THE KNIGHTS OF ST. JOHN.

Boisgelin, himself a Knight of Malta, gives the following authentic copy of the Oath of Profession, from the original text, which every Candidate took at his reception into the Order:—

VOW OF THE KNIGHTS OF ST. JOHN.

"Io N. faccio voto e prometto a Dio Omnipotente, ed alla Beata Maria sempre Vergine, Madre di Dio, ed a San Giovanni Battista d'osservare perpetuamente, con l'ajuta di Dio, vera obedienza a qualunque superiore che mi sera data da Dio e dalla nostra religione, e di più vivere senza proprio e d'osservare castità."

VOW OF THE TEMPLARS,

VOTUM,
IN NOMINE DEI PATRIS + ET FILII + ET SPIRITUS SANCTI.

EGO,

ORDINIS TEMPLI MILITIAE SANCTAE MEMETIPSUM AD PRAESENS ET IN OEVUM DE-VOVENS, LIBERE SOLEMNITERQUE OBEDIEN-TIAE, PAUPERTATIS, ET CASTITATIS, SICUT ET FRATERNITATIS, HOSPITALITATIS ET PRAELIATIONIS VOTUM SUSCIPERE PROFITEOR;

Quo voto firmam et non quassabilem edico voluntatem, ad Religionis Christianae, Ordinis Templi, Commilitonumque causam, tutelam et honorem, maximamque illustrationem, et ad Templi Sepulchrique Domini Nostri Jesu Christi Palestinae, Orientisque terrae et Patrum dominiorum recuperationem, gladium, vires, vitamque et singula alia mea impendendi,

Regulae S. P. Bernardi, Chartae transmissionis, regulis, legibus, decretis, singulisque aliis actis, secundum Ordinis Statuta emissis me submittendi: nullos Equites creaturus, nullosve titulos aut gradus ritusque et usus Ordinis proditurus, nisi patuerit ex Statutis licentia: omni denique modo, sive in Ordinis domibus sive foras et in quocumque vitae, statu Supremo Magistro, omnibusque et singulis in Militia superioribus absolute obediturus.

Sic Fratres meos Equites Templi, Sororesque Equitissas in charitate habendi, ut ipsos, Fratrumque Viduas et liberos, sicut et Sororum liberos, gladio, concilio, copiis, opibus, auctoritate, singulisque rebus meis adjuvem, illosque semper et ubique, nullo casu excepto, cuivis Commilitonum Templi non consorti praeferam;

Pios peregrinos tuendi; captivorum propter crucem, infirmorumque et pauperum subsidio simul et solatio inserviendi:

Infideles et incredulos, exemplo, virtute, bonis operibus, alloquiisque suasoriis oppugnandi: in In-

FIDELES AUTEM ET INCREDULOS GLADIO CRUCEM AGGRE-DIENTES, PROPTER CRUCEM GLADIO PRAELIANDI:

AB OMNI IMPUDICITIA ABHORRENDI, ET AD NULLAM CARNIS OPERAM, NISI DEBITAM, ET TANTUM CUM UXORE LEGITIMA ACCEDENDI:

TANDEM APUD SINGULAS QUAS ADIBO GENTES, IP-SARUM, SALVO RELIGIONIS ORDINISQUE JURE, LEGIBUS ET MORIBUS OBTEMPERANDI: GENTIBUS VERO HOSPITALITATE ET AMICITIA ORDINEM COLENTIBUS, CUIS ET EQUITIS FI-DELISSIMI SACRA OFFICIA PRAESTANDI.

HAEC SIC, CORAM EQUITIBUS (HUICCE CONVENTUI ADSTANTIBUS) VOVEO, ALTA VOCE DICO, ET VOVERE PROFITEOR. QUOD VOTUM SANGUINE MEO SUBSIGNO ET CONFIRMO, ATQUE IN TABULAS (CONVENTUALES) ITERUM SCRIBO ET SUBSIGNO, SUBSIGNANTIBUS SUPRA DICTIS TESTIBUS.

GLORIA PATRI + ET FILIO + ET SPRITUI SANCTO, + AMEN.

N.B.—The above Vow is always signed with the inter-pretation explained in the text annexed to it.

LE TRÉSOR

Inventaire des Chartre, Statuts, Reliques et Insignes composant le Trésor sacré de l'Ordre du Temple, extrait de la minute du procès-verbal qui en a été dressé le 14[e.] jour de la lune de Tab., l'an de l'Ordre 692, du Magister le 6[e.] (18 mai 1810.)

Ire. PIÈCE DU TRÉSOR.

La chartre de transmission (par J. M. *Larmenius*), écrite en deux colonnes et demie sur une très-grande feuille de parchemin, ornée, suivant le goût du temps, de dessins gothiques architecturaux, de lettres fleuronnées, coloriées, dorées et argentées, dont la première offre un chevalier appuyé sur un bouclier armorie de la croix de l'Ordre.

Au haut, en tête, est peinte la croix conventuelle dans la forme aulique.

Au bas est le sceau de la milice, suspendu par des lacs de parchemin.

Les acceptations par les Grands-Maîtres commencent vers le milieu de la troisième colonne, se continuant à la troisième, et finissant aux deux tiers inférieurs de la marge à droite.

IIe. PIÈCE.

L'archétype des Statuts de l'an de l'Ordre (587,) transcrits à la main sur vingt-sept feuilles de papier, reliés en un volume petit in-folio, couvert en velours cramoisi, doublé en satin *idem*, doré sur tranche.— Cette pièce signée Philippus (*d'Orléans.*)

IIIe. PIÈCE.

Un petit reliquaire de cuivre, en forme d'église gothique, contenant, dans un suaire de lin, quatre fragmens d'os brulés, extraits du bûcher des martyrs de l'Ordre.

IVe. PIÈCE.

Une épée de fer (cruciforme) surmontée d'une boule, et présumée avoir servi au G.-M. J. *Molay.*

V^e. PIÈCE.

Un casque de fer, à visière, armorié de dauphins et damastiqué en or, présumé être celui de *Guy*, dauphin d'Auvergne.

VIe. PIÈCE.

Un ancien éperon de cuivre doré.

VIIe. PIÈCE.

Une patène de bronze, dans l'intérieur de laquelle est gravée une main étendue, dont le petit doigt et l'annulaire sont repliés dans la paume.

VIIIe. PIÈCE.

Une paix en bronze doré, représentant Saint-Jean sous une arcade gothique.

IXe. PIÈCE.

Trois sceaux gothiques de bronze en forme ovale pointue, et de grandeur différente, désignés dans les Statuts sous les noms de *sceau du G.-M. Jean, sceau du chevalier croisé, et sceau de Saint-Jean.*

X^e. PIÈCE.

Un haut de crosse d'ivoire et trois mitres d'étoffe,

l'une en or, brodée en soie, et deux en argent, brodées en perles, ayant servi aux cérémonies de l'Ordre.

XIe. PIÈCE.

Le baucéant en laine blanche, à la croix de l'Ordre.

XIIe. et dernière PIÈCE.

Le drapeau de guerre, en laine blanche, à quatre raies noires.

MANIFESTO BY THE LATE REGENT ON HIS SUCCESSION,

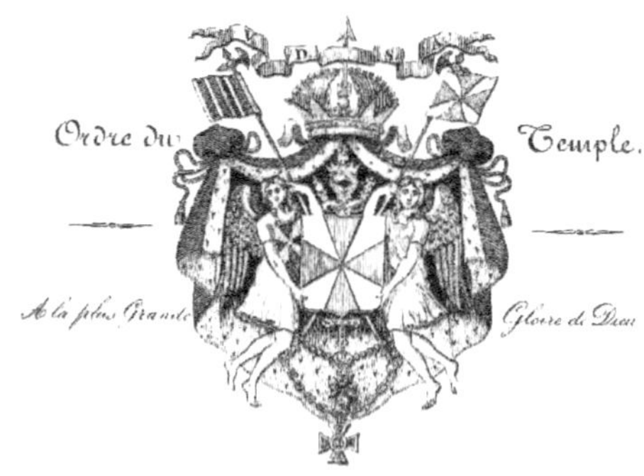

**Ordre du Temple
A la plus Grande Gloire de Dieu.**

Guillaume-Sidney,

Par la Grace de Dieu, et la désignation Testamentaire
du dernier Grand-Maître.

Prince Magistral, Régent de l'Ordre du Temple;

A Tous Ceux qui ces Présentes, Verront:

Salut.

Vu, l'Article 38 des Statuts de l'Ordre du Temple, et le 3me paragraphe de la Charte de transmission;
Vu, les Articles 13, 15, 16 et suivans desdits Status;
Considérant, que l'état de haute civilisation des diverses Nations Européennes et principalement de la France, ou se trouve le siège Magistral, permet toute Réunion du Convent Général, sans qu'il puisse en résulter le moindre danger pour les Chevaliers;
Considérant, que les temps sont venus de rendre au Convent général tous les droits dont il a joui jusques au G. M. Jacques de Molay, (à qui scient honneur et gloire), et de faire rentrer dans de sages et constitutionnelles limites la puissance du Magistère;
Considérant, qu'une reforme prudente et réfléchie des Statuts, dans les parties qui ne sont plus en harmonie avec la Charte de transmission, les moeurs du siècle et la règle, est le moyen le plus efficace de rendre possible l'accomplissement des hautes destinées auxquelles l'Ordre du Temple est appelé;
Le conseil privé entendu;
Nous avons décrété et décrétons ce qui suit:

ARTICLE PREMIER.

Le Convent Général de l'Ordre du Temple est Convoqué pour le dix Novembre, 1838.

Article **II.**

Immédiatement après sa réunion, le Convent général devra se prononcer sur la présentation du Prince Magistral Régent, désigné par Bernard Raymond (à qui soient honneur et gloire) pour lui succéder en qualité de Grand Maître de l'Ordre du Temple.

Article **III.**

En tête du Commentarium sera placé la revision du Chapitre IV et de tous les Articles des Statuts qui ont des connexions avec ce Chapitre.

Article **IV.**

Il sera ouvert à la Sécretairerie Magistrale un Registre destiné à l'inscription des propositions faites pour être présentées au Convent général, et qui seront insérées au Commentarium, conformément aux Statuts.

Soit, le présent décret, expédié, enregistré et scellé par qui et a qui de droit; adressé spécialement au Grand Connétable, au Gouverneur général et au Grand Maître des Dépêches, qui sont chargés de son exécution;

Soit aussi, ledit Décret, envoyé par lettres communicatoires, 1°, au Prieur de chaque Convent, pour être porté à la connaissance de tous les Chevaliers de son

obédience, 2°, et personnellement, aux Chevaliers qui
ne feraient partie d'aucune Maison de l'Ordre.

Signé Guillaume Sidney
De par S. A. le Prince Magistral, Régent de l'Ordre.
Le Grand Précepteur, Ministre Secrétaire Magistral,
Signé Réné Léon De Sud-Europe.
Enregistré en la grande Sénéchaussée, le 3 Mai 1838.
Le Ministre Grand Sénéchal,
Signé, Eugène De France.
Scellé en la grande Chancellerie, le même jour,
Le Grand-Précepteur, Ministre Grand Chancelier,
Signé, Felix De Nord-Afrique.
Vu par le Grand-Connétable;
Signé F. Sébastien Louis De Bauvais.
Vu par le Gouverneur Général;
Signé F. Fréchot.
Vu par le Grand Maître des Dépêches;
Signé F. E. Louber.

Pour copie conforme:

Le Grand Précepteur, Ministre Secrétaire Magistral.
F. Réné Léon De Sud-Europe.

Donné à Paris, en notre résidence Magistrale, le 1er du mois de Mai, de l'an de N. S. J. C. 1838, 720°. de l'Ordre.

Signé ✠ F. ✠ Guillaume Sidney

De par S. A. le Prince Magistral, Régent de l'Ordre.

Le Grand Précepteur, Ministre Secrétaire Magistral,

Signé ✠ F. ✠ Réné Léon De Sud-Europe.

Enregistré en la grande Sénéchaussée, le 3 Mai 1838.

Le Ministre Grand Sénéchal,

Signé, ✠ F. ✠ Eugène De France.

Scellé en la grande Chancellerie, le même jour,

Le Grand-Précepteur, Ministre Grand Chancelier,

Signé, ✠ F. ✠ Félix De Nord-Afrique.

Vu par le Grand-Connétable ; Signé ✠ F. Sébastien Louis De Beauvais.

Vu par le Gouverneur Général ; Signé F. ✠ Fréchot.

Vu par le Grand Maître des Dépêches, Signé ✠ F. E. Loubert ✠.

Pour copie conforme :

Le Grand Précepteur, Ministre Secrétaire Magistral.

✠ F. ✠ Réné Léon De Sud-Europe.

DISCOURS DE L'AMIRAL SIR SIDNEY SMITH,

AU CONVENT GENERAL LE 27 JANVIER 1837.

S. A. le Lieutenant-Général d'Asie demande la parole.
Ce vénérable frère s'exprime ainsi qu'il suit.

"Sérénissime Grand-Maître, et vous tous mes nobles frères:

"Justement et infiniment sensible à l'honneur qui m'a été conféré, par suite de ma nomination, à la haute dignité de Lieutenant-Général d'Asie, je dois vous en témoigner toute ma reconnaissance.

"A mon âge avancé, je puis prétendre à être considéré comme exempt d'ambition : je vois par conséquent dans cet acte de la haute confiance du Grand-Maître, une charge onéreuse et un lourd fardeau, plutôt qu'un avantage : mais, je l'accepte avec respect. Mes soins et mes efforts constants seront toujours employés pour prouver que je n'ai pas fait en vain le serment de fidélité et de soumission à l'ordre et à son chef suprême.

"Je vois dans cette nomination une preuve de la vraie libéralité du Grand-Maître éclairé de cet ordre, essentiellement cosmopolite, où toutes les nations chrétiennes se confondent et co-opèrent ensemble pour le maintien de la paix du monde et de l'harmonie entre les sectes religieuses, par la tolérance, la charité et la protection pour les pèlerins en Terre Sainte, contre les pirates et brigands; premier but de sa fondation, qui précéda les autres ordres de la chevalerie moderne, ordres qui *n'ont été* et ne *sont* que ses *imitateurs* : car le notre ne demande que l'occasion de remplir son devoir sacré. Aussi est-ce avec une vive satisfaction que je vois enfin un Grand-Maître apprécier l'importance de l'ordre, *et pour la première fois, appeler pour un de ses lieutenants, je ne dis pas un anglais, mais un templier de la langue d'Angleterre. Honneur au Grand-Maître qui a fait un tel acte, et qui montre ainsi à toutes les nations, que toutes ont des droits égaux à remplir les diverses charges du Temple* : Honneur à ce chef qui a si longtemps et si loyalement conservé le feu sacré, et les traditions, malgré les orages et les persécutions, suite d'une révolution dont l'origine remonte pour nous, à *Philippe-le-Bel* et au *Pape Clement V.* Mais espérons qu'enfin nous rentrerons dans tous nos droits ; et qu'au lieu de dresser la tente magistrale dans une langue excentrique, un jour nous la dresserons au lieu de notre création, dans la ville qui nous appartient, dans la *sainte Jérusalem* !

"Honneur aux très nobles chevaliers qui se sont montrés pénétrés du sentiment de leurs devoirs, et ont donné constamment des preuves qu'ils sont incapables d'oublier leur serment de fidélité et d'obéissance !......

"J'ai déjà communiqué verbalement à S. A. E., devant témoins, ce que j'ai consigné dans mon testament, la disposition formelle, pour la restitution au chef du Temple, d'une croix de l'ordre qui est très ancienne, à en juger par sa forme et la monture des pierres, laquelle croix a appartenu à un de ses Grand-Maîtres, et fut du temps des croisades portée dans la guerre sainte par le roi d'Angleterre *Richard* Ier, dit *Cœur-de-Lion*. Ce roi l'a laissée en dépôt entre les mains de l'archevêque de Chypre lors de son départ de cette ile, dont il était Souverain par conquête. J'ai été personnellement décoré de cette croix en 1799, par les mains du dix-huitième archevêque, successeur du dépositaire, qui l'a placé sur ma poitrine, en reconnaissance de la réussite de mes efforts, pour rétablir la paix et la protection due à la population chrétienne de l'île, contre l'insurrection des troupes Asiatiques qui avaient assassiné leur chef, appelé le *Patrona Bey*, et commençaient déjà à se livrer au pillage et au massacre des habitants : désastres que j'ai empêchés par ma présence au milieu de ces furieux, sans armes, le firman du Sultan *Selim* en main, et par la nomination d'un successeur *à Patrona Bey*, en vertu de l'autorité suprême qui m'avait été déléguée dans le temps par la Porte Ottomane, sur les forces combinées de terre et de mer dans le Levant.

"L'autorité qui maintenant m'est déléguée par le

sérénissime grand-maitre sur le continent d'Asie, pourra en temps et lieu être employée utilement pour protéger la population chrétienne de ces contrées, et le maintien de la hiérarchie de l'ordre. Croyez, que pour la plus grande gloire du Temple, je me ferai un devoir d'employer l'influence que les antécédents m'ont donnée. *Les templiers fidèles peuvent compter sur moi.*"

Le grand-maitre exprime au lieutenant-général d'Asie, les sentiments dont lui et ses frères sont animés pour un Chevalier qui a conquis l'admiration du monde par ses hauts faits maritimes, et a mérité par ses vertus sociales et templières, l'estime et l'affection de tous ses frères. Le grand-maitre lui donne au nom de l'ordre l'accolade fraternelle.

Le Convent Général ordonne que le discours de l'Amiral *Sir Sidney Smith* soit inséré textuellement au procès-verbal.

INVESTITURE AS A KNIGHT COMMANDER OF THE BATH,

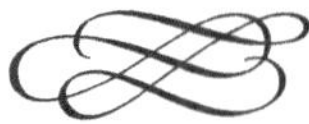

The following account from the pen of the learned Biographer of the gallant Admiral, of the Investiture of Sir Sidney Smith, as a Knight Commander of the Bath, by his contemporary and brother in arms, the great and illustrious Wellington, and the "very extraordinary" document which follows, will, no doubt, be read with much interest:

Towards the termination of this year, 1815, our officer was honoured, in a most particular manner, by his Sovereign.

His Grace the Duke of Wellington having received the gracious commands of his Royal Highness the Prince Regent of the United Kingdoms, through his Royal Highness the Duke of York, Grand-master of the most honourable order of the Bath, to invest Vice-Admiral Sir William Sidney Smith, Knight-commander-grand-cross of the Royal Military Order of the

Sword, with the insignia of commander of the aforesaid, his Grace fixed on the 29th of December for the performance of the ceremony, which took place accordingly at the Palace Elisée-Bourbon, the Knights-grand-crosses, Knights-commanders, and Companions being present, as also his Grace the Duke of Richmond and the Right Honourable the Earl of Hardwick, both Knights of the most noble Order of the Garter.

At six o'clock the Commander elect arrived at the palace, and being conducted and supported into the presence of the noble Duke representing the Sovereign on the occasion, by the two junior grand-crosses, Sir James Kempt and Sir Henry Colville, after the usual reverences in advancing, (the Commander elect being already a Knight, the usual ceremony of dubbing him as such was formally dispensed with,) his Grace proceeded, according to the order of his Royal Highness the Grand-Master, which he first read, and invested the Commander with the insignia of the Order: after which his Grace embraced Sir Sidney Smith twice most cordially, with every demonstration of the feelings of esteem and regard, feelings which the Knights, Grand-crosses, and Commanders, many of whom had served in Egypt as his juniors in rank, also testified; and it certainly may be said to be a proud day for England when such a scene took place in the evacuated palace of Buonaparte, between these two British officers of the two services, one of whom first checked, and the other of whom finally closed, the career of that ambitious chieftain.

The banquet being announced, his Grace desired his Excellency the British ambassador, Sir Charles Stuart, G.C.B., to conduct the new Knight Commander to the hall of the same, where the members of the Order, including some foreigners of distinction, amongst whom were Don Michael Alava, General Muffling, and Count Demetrius Valsamachi, a nobleman of the Ionian Islands, were entertained most sumptuously in the usual style of the Duke's elegant hospitality.

After the health of the King and Prince Regent had been drunk, the Duke gave the health of "Sir Sidney Smith:" the company hereupon rose, and followed his Grace's example in greeting the new Commander with the most cordial acclamations. When silence was restored, Sir Sidney Smith rose, and addressed the company nearly as follows:—

"My Lords, noble Knights, Grand Crosses, Commanders, and Companions!—I should not do justice to my feelings, were I not to endeavour to express them in returning you my thanks for the honour you have done me by this reception: at the same time, I feel I cannot do justice to them by any mode of expression I can make use of.

"The language of *compliment* must die on the lips of any man in the presence of the Duke of Wellington; first, from the inadequacy of all language to express what every man must feel when speaking of such a highly distinguished chief; next, from the recollection of the noble simplicity of his character which disdains it. It will, I trust, be readily believed, that I must be most truly gratified to be invested by a knight of such high renown and glorious achievements; and the more so in this *particular place*, and in an assembly of so many illustrious and highly distinguished Knights-Commanders and Companions. A combination of circumstances, which could only happen in the present times, and are mainly owing to the successful result of the battle of Waterloo. Noble and illustrious Knights, I beg you to accept the expression of my humble thanks for the honour you have done me."

The Duke of Wellington having acceded to Sir Sidney Smith's request to be allowed to propose a toast to the company, he proceeded to say—"I beg leave to call to remembrance that this day (the 29th of December) is the anniversary of a re-union of illustrious knights of various orders, which took place at Vienna, where many Sovereigns were present, and when the toast I shall have the honour to propose to you was drunk by them with a manifestation of their conviction, that the object of it intimately concerned knighthood as such, in all nations. I beg leave to propose the health and deliverance of the *white Slaves in the Barbary States*."

The toast was received with the most marked approbation, and drunk with the usual demonstrations thereof, by three times three regular and hearty cheers, when the company adjourned to the ballroom, preceded, on the indication of the Duke of

Wellington, by the new Knight-Commander, supported by his Britannic Majesty's ambassador, in the same order as on entrance, where a brilliant assembly of ladies, English, French, Spanish, Russian, &c. &c. continued to increase till a late hour; his Royal Highness the Duke of Berry, the French, and the foreign ministers, were also present, and all joined in cordial congratulations of, and compliments to, the cosmopolite chieftain, President of the Knights Liberators of the white slaves in Africa; who, we observed, was decorated with the various orders of the nations he has contributed by his endeavours to release from the yoke of the former inhabitants of the palace where this extraordinary assembly was held; then a prisoner on the top of a rock in the Southern Atlantic. These circumstances reminded the Parisians of the prophetic inscriptions left by Sidney Smith on the window shutter of the Temple prison, when he escaped, of which many copies were taken and are now again in circulation, and read with great interest since the accomplishment has taken place: we have been favoured with a translation, of which we give our readers a copy, the original having been in French, and respected by various successive guardians of the tower, till the Prince de Rohan, afterwards Duke de Rohan, subsequently a prisoner in that tower, removed it for its preservation, and we are assured he now possesses it.

"SIDNEY SMITH TO BUONAPARTE."

"Fortune's wheel makes strange revolutions, it must be confessed; but for the term revolution to be applicable, the term should be a complete one, for a half turn is not a revolution; (see the Dictionary of the Academy;) you are at present as high as you can mount. Well! I don't envy you your fortunate situation, for I am better off than you; I am as low in the career of ambition as a man can descend; so that let fortune turn her wheel ever so little, and as she is capricious, turn it she will, I must necessarily mount, and you as necessarily must descend. I do not make this remark to you to cause you any chagrin; on the contrary, with the intent to bring you the same consolation I have at present when you shall arrive at the same point where I am; yes! the same point; you will inhabit this prison, why not as well as I? I did not think of such a thing any more than you do at present, before I found myself brought hither. In party wars 'tis a crime in the eyes of opponents for a man to do his duty well; you do yours now, and consequently you by so much irritate your enemies; you will answer me.

"'I fear not their combined hatred, the voice of the people is declared for me, I serve them well:' that is all very good talking; sleep in quiet, you'll very soon learn what one gains by serving such a master, whose inconstancy will perhaps punish you *for all the good* you do him. 'Whoever,' (says an ancient author, Pausanias Atticus,) 'puts his entire confidence in public favour, never passes his life without pain and trouble, and seldom comes to a good end.'

"In fact, I need not prove to you that you will come here and read these lines, because here you must be to read them. You will certainly have this chamber, because it is the best, and the keeper, who is a very civil good sort of man, will, of course, treat you as well as he does me."

N. B.—These lines having appeared in the Parisian papers in 1799, and having been put into Buonaparte's hands at Cairo, on his return from his unsuccessful Syrian expedition, where he was foiled and worsted by the writer of them, he exclaimed, 'It is very extraordinary;' and on his return to Paris, fearing the accomplishment of the remainder of the prediction, after having procured through Regnauld de St. Jean d'Angely the sight of a copy in the hands of Baruel Beauvert, he forthwith ordered the building to be levelled to the ground.

After this display of his country's gratitude to Sir Sidney Smith, which became so much the more enhanced, as it may be said to have taken place almost in the presence of so many Sovereigns, Sir Sidney had little else to do but to enjoy his richly-merited rewards, the universal admiration, and the approbation of his own mind, ever active in doing good, not only for his country, but for the whole human race.

He prosecuted with ardour his plans for the abolition of white slavery, even after the destruction of the pirates' nest in Algiers.

DEATH AND FUNERAL OF ADMIRAL SIR WILLIAM SIDNEY SMITH, G.C.B. &C. &C. &C.

Sir William Sidney Smith died on Friday Morning, the 26th May 1840, at his residence, No. 9, Rue d'Aguisseau, in the 76th year of his age. Honoured by his Sovereign, and decorated with the Orders of almost every State in Europe, he was, in private life, beloved and respected by all who had the pleasure of his friendship or acquaintance. His chivalrous and lofty bearing, his cheerful and animated conversation, his unbounded fund of anecdote, suavity of temper, and invariable benevolence, rendered him a most welcome and instructive companion.—It has been truly written by his Biographer,

"Than Sir Sidney Smith, no one ever inscribed on

the pages of History, and even of Romance, more emphatically deserved the title of Hero."

The mortal remains of this Gallant and Illustrious Admiral were interred, May 29, in the Cimetiére de l' Est, or Eastern Division of the Great Cemetery of Pére la Chaise. The body was taken from his late residence in the Rue d'Aguisseau to the English Episcopal Church in the same street, followed by his relatives, William and Herbert Smith, Esquires, Nephews, Captain Arabin, and —— St. Clair, Esquire, Sons-in-law of the deceased, with Vice Admiral Sir Charles Rowley, Bart. Lieut.-General Lord Aylmer, General Count Excelmans, Peer of France, and the French Admiral Bergeret, as supporters of the Pall, besides many of the principal English residents in Paris, among whom were several officers of high rank in the British Navy. —The introductory part of the service was performed in the Church by the Right Reverend Bishop Luscombe, and two assistants, and the body was then borne to the Cemetery, attended by a long cortége of mourning and private carriages. On the Coffin was placed the Hat, Sword, and Uniform of the deceased, and on a cushion his epaulettes and numerous orders. Over the foot of the coffin was spread the British Union Jack. At the conclusion of the burial service, which was most impressively read by Bishop Luscombe, three orations were delivered—the first by Monsieur Jullien, of Paris, who gave a short but comprehensive recapitulation of the services of Sir Sidney, from his first entering the British Navy at the age of 13, and also expatiated largely on his amiable and philanthrophic qualities. The next speaker, M. Caille, Advocate of the Cour Royale of Paris, after pronouncing a general panegyric on the character of the deceased as a warrior, proceeded to eulogise him for his active and generous exertion in promoting the objects of several philanthropic societies of which he was a member, and to which his advice, his practical and scientific acquirements, and his inventions, were so invaluable. Both speakers were loud in their praise of Sir Sidney, for his having been almost the first to interfere for the suppression of European slavery in Africa, and for his indefatigable and strenuous exertions in that humane cause. The third gentleman, M. Raoul, Advocat of the Court of Cassation, spoke in a similar strain of eulogium of the character of Sir Sidney as a citizen of the world, ever ready to aid the cause of humanity. No stronger testimony to his worth could, however, have been shewn, than to hear his eulogium pronounced solely by members of a Nation against which, in his career of arms, he had so successfully and gloriously fought. Sir Sidney Smith was Prince Magistral and Regent of the Order of the Temple, and a Member of the Legion of Honour.

The following two Discourses pronounced upon the melancholy occasion, were, in the kindest and most handsome manner, contributed by M. Jullien, the learned author of many valuable works.—

DISCOURS PRONONCÉ AUX FUNÉRAILLES DE L'AMIRAL SIR SIDNEY SMITH,

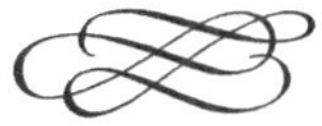

PAR M. JULLIEN, DE PARIS,

Son ancien ami et son Collègue, comme membre et président honoraire de plusieurs Sociétés Savantes ou Philantropiques, le 29 Mai 1840.

Messieurs,

L'homme respectable auquel nous venons adresser un dernier adieu, ne fut pas seulement un marin et un guerrier célèbre; il fut surtout un ami constant, dévoué et chevaleresque de l'humanité. Dans sa longue et aventureuse carrière qu'il a parcourue avec tant d'éclat, il s'est moins distingué encore par sa brillante valeur que par une loyauté et une générosité qui lui ont conquis les coeurs, même de ses ennemis. Né a Londres le 21 Juin 1764, entré au Service en 1777, avant l'âge de 13 ans, comme simple novice (élève de marine,) a bord d'une frégate stationnée sur les côtes de l'Amérique, pendant la guerre de l'indépendance, il passa, en 1779, sur le Sandwich, vaisseau de 90 canons, sur lequel l'Amiral Sir George Bridges Rodney arbora son pavillon de Commandement-en-Chef, et fit voile, le jour de noël de cette même année, pour Gibraltar, et ensuite pour les Indes Occidentales, Sidney Smith fut successivement Lieutenant de vaisseau et Capitaine de corvette. Il prit part à tous les combats qui eurent lieu dans cet hémisphère jusqu'à la paix de 1783.

En 1788, Sidney Smith passa en Suède, alors en guerre avec la Russie, ostensiblement comme volontaire auxiliaire, mais en réalité comme Aide-de-Camp honoraire et intime du roi Gustave III. Après avoir rendu, en cette qualité, les plus brillant et les plus utiles services à la Suède, il reçut des mains mêmes de ce monarque chevaleresque, la décoration de première classe de l'ordre de l'epée. A cette époque, ces distinctions honorifiques n'étaient point prodiguées et prostituées, comme elles l'ont été depuis, et elles avaient un véritable prix, n'étant accordées qu'au mérite et aux services réels.

En 1793, le jeune Smith se rendit comme volontaire en Turquie, où il conduisit avec lui plusieurs constructeurs de vaisseaux. Peu après, il était chargé d'un commandement dans la Croisière Anglaise sur les côtes de France. Le 18 Avril 1796, ayant abordé un vaisseau Français à la hauteur du Ilaîre, obligé par le courant de remonter la Seine, il fut fait prisonnier par des forces supérieures qui l'attaquèrent; puis amené à Paris, ou il resta deux ans dans le prisons de l'Abbaye et du Temple. Echappé de sa prison par l'intervention d'amis dévoués, il rejoignit la flotte Anglaise en 1798. La même année, appelé à commander les forces auxiliaires que La Grande-Bretagne mettait à la disposition de la Turquie, où son frère Sir Spencer Smith, était Ministre Plénipotentiaire, auprès de là Porte Ottomane, il se trouve le 1 Mars 1799, jusqu'au 20 Mai suivant, au siège mémorable de Saint Jean d'Acre, et co-opère puissamment à la défense de cette place.

Nous ne devons, en présence d'un cercueil, rappeler que des souvenirs compatibles avec notre unanime sympathie pour notre illustre ami, Bornons-nous à dire que Sidney Smith se montra grand et magnanime envers les Français faits prisonniers ; il sut les garantir, par son énergique volonté, des violences et de la barbarie Turques; il mérita leur estime et leur affection; et la loyauté Française aime à reconnaître que sa conduite, lors même qu'il était l'allié de nos ennemis, fut noble et généreuse envers ceux que le sort des armes mettait en sa puissance. Les généraux Kleber et Desaix, qui entrèrent en négociation avec lui après le départ de Bonaparte, ont apprécié sa droiture et son humanité, et lui ont rendu justice.

Sidney Smith, après avoir sauvé la vie de nos compatriotes, rendit intactes aux savants de l'expédition les caisses contenant les papiers et les cartes qui devaient servir à écrire l'histoire de la campagne d'Egypte. Aussi, à la paix le gouvernement Français, sur la proposition de la commission de l'institut Egyptien lui a offert un exemplaire de ce magnifique ouvrage, comme un témoignage de la reconnaissance publique.

Après les événements d'Egypte et de Syrée, où Sidney Smith avait contribué à ménager à l'armée Française des conditions honorables pour revenir dans sa patrie, il quitta lui-même les parages de l'Orient, et se rendit en Angleterre où il fut élu membre de la Chambre des Communes, par la ville de Rochester, en 1802.

Nous le voyons reparaître, en 1803, avec un commandement sur les côtes de la France et de la Hollande. En 1807, il commande la flotte chargée de défendre la Sicile. En 1806, il est envoyé à Constantinople où il force les Dardanelles, au mois d'Octobre 1807, il commande les forces Anglaises mises à la disposition du Portugal ; et le 29 Novembre suivant, une partie de sa flotte accompagne au Brésil la famille royale, qui va chercher au-delà des mers un asile dans ses possessions Américaines.

Dans ses relations avec les Rois et avec les princes souverains, comme avec les peuples et dans tous les pays où le conduisit sa destinée aventureuse, Sidney Smith contracta d'honorables et d'illustres amitiés. Ce fut principalement en 1814, au Congrès de Vienne, qu'il fixa l'attention de tous les grands personnages réunie alors pour poster les vases de la Paix Européenne, et qu'il reçut de tous sans exception les hommages, d'une estime respectueuse. Il conçut alors la pensée philanthropique de fonder, avec le concours des Monarques alliés, et de tous les hommes de bien qui partageaient ses vues, une *institution anti-pirate*, en *association des chevaliers libérateurs des esclaves blancs et noirs en Afrique*. Car, il avait souvent déploré, dans ses commandement sur les différents points de la Méditerranée, les actes cruels de la piraterie barbaresque, trop longtemps tolérée par les puissances Chrétiennes, et il s'était promis d'y mettre un terme. Plus de cent noms illustres remplirent les listes de souscription qu'il avait ouvertes. Il entretint, pendant plusieurs années, une vaste et active correspondance, au moyen de laquelle il contribua puissamment à faire cesser les malheurs d'un grand nombre de victimes, des actes de piraterie qui jusqu'alors s'étaient commis impunément et presque librement sous les yeux de l'Europe civilisée.

Pendant les 25 années de paix générale qui ont précédé sa mort, le grand homme de guerre que nous pleurons aujourd'hui se montra constamment homme pacifique et bienfaisant, véritable cosmopolite, ami sincère de l'humanité, en prennent ce mot dans sa plus complète acception.

Par une singularité nouvelle de sa destinée, Sidney-Smith meurt en France, où il reçoit les regrets et les hommages de ses compatriotes, et de ses concitoyens d'adoption, au moment même où l'Angleterre, sa patrie, restitue à la France les cendres de Napoléon. La nation Anglaise paie un tribute d'admiration à ce même Empereur qu'elle n'a cessé de combattre pendant sa vie. La terre Française reçoit les dépouilles mortelles de l'Amiral Britannique qui employa longtemps contre elle ses talents et son courage, qui depuis a consacré 25 années à servir, au milieu des Français et avec leur co-opération, la cause sacrée de l'humanité et celle du malheur.

Au nombre des titre de gloire de l'Amiral, nous ne devons pas omettre la louable persévérance avec laquelle il s'est occupé de perfectionner les moyens de sauvetage et sa grande part à la fondation de la société générale des naufrages, qui a donné un plus grand développement à ses vues bienfaisantes. Ainsi les passions humaines s'éteignent en présence d'un tombeau. Ainsi les nations abjurent de cruelles et injustes antipathies qui les ont trop longtemps divisées. Ainsi tous les hommes de bien, quelle que soit leur terre natale, se réunissent pour honorer l'homme qui, par ses vertus et ses actions, a servi avec dévouement les grands intérêts de la famille humaine.

DISCOURS PRONONCÉ SUR LA TOMBE DE SIR WILLIAM SIDNEY SMITH,

AMIRAL DE LA FLOTTE ROUGE D'ANGLETERRE,

Lors de ses obsèques, dans le cimetière de l'Est, à Paris, le 29 Mai 1840, par M. CAILLE,
Avocat à la Cour Royale de Paris.

Messieurs,

Invité depuis quelques instants seulement, par la famille de l'Amiral William Sidney Smith, á exprimer de justes regrets sur sa tombe, je ne puis apporter qu'un bien faible tribut d'admiration à sa mémoire, surtout après l'éloge que vient de prononcer au nom de l'Ordre du Temple, dont cet illustre Anglais était le régent, l'un des dignitaires de cet ordre, et lorsqu'une notice historique de sa vie vous a été présentée par l'un des littérateurs les plus distingués de la France.

L'histoire transmettra à la postérité les exploits du célèbre marin, de l'habile négociateur, du généreux philanthrope, dont nous déplorons la perte. C'est exclusivement sous le rapport moral et philosophique que j'essaierai de vous retracer quelques épisodes de sa carrière entièrement consacrée au bonheur de ses semblables, et l'influence politique qu'il exerça sur les états, avec lesquels il fut mis en rapport par son gouvernement.

Sidney-Smith, comme vous le savez, comptait déjà dix-huit années de services militaires distingués, lorsque, à l'âge de trente-quatre ans, il fut chargé par le ministère Anglais, en qualité de commodore, de la station maritime de l'Archipel du Levant, en 1798 ; c'est-à-dire à l'époque de la conquête de l'Egypte, par l'armée de la république Française, sous les ordres du général Bonaparte.

Je ne vous peindrai pas sa lutte héroïque avec le géant du siècle, à Saint-Jean-d'Acre, dont il fit lever le siège après soixante jours de tranchée : je me hâte de vous signaler un service qui devait être incalculable dans ses conséquences politiques, et que Sidney-Smith rendit à la sublime Porte, dont il releva le courage par ses succès: il sut profiter du crédit obtenu par sa victoire de Saint-Jean-d'Acre, auprès du sultan Selim III, et de Kléber, général de l'armée Française en Egypte, depuis le retour de Bonaparte en France, pour négocier le fameux traité d'El-Arich, du 24 janvier 1801, traité qu'il considérait comme le préliminaire de la paix entre les puissances belligérantes. Il y stipula que l'armée française évacuerait l'Egypte, avec armes et bagages, et serait transportée en France.

Sidney-Smith signa ce traité avec les pleins pouvoirs du ministère Britannique, dont il était revêtu : le grand-vizir et le général Kléber le signèrent, au nom de leurs gouvernements respectifs.

Je ne puis trop insister, messieurs, sur cette époque où Sidney-Smith arbora l'olive de la paix entre trois camps ennemis; il avait prévu les nouvelles destinées de la France, et sa haute sagesse avait préféré de traiter avec elle, dans l'intérêt de la Sublime Porte, et de gouvernement Britannique lui-même, et surtout dans l'intérêt de l'humanité, plutôt que de courir la chance faillible des combats.

Mais le ministère Anglais, qui ne lui avait donné qu'à regret des pouvoirs et des instructions pacifiques, informé que l'armée du grand vizir était forte de 80,000 hommes, tandis que celle de Kléber ne l'était que de 8000, crut l'occasion favorable d'anéantir la puissance Française en Egypte, il refusa de ratifier le traité d'El-Arich, et osa donner l'ordre à l'amiral Keith d'exiger que l'armée Française mît bas les armes et se rendît prisonnière de guerre. Sidney-Smith fut profondément affligé de cette violation des lois de la guerre et du droit des gens.

Dés-lors les hostilités recommencèrent. L'armée Française combattit avec ce sentiment de l'indignation qui décuple le courage: elle défit entièrement l'armée ottomane á Héliopolis. Le grand-vizir, qui la commandait, ne dut son salut qu'à la fuite, en laissant aux vainqueurs ses bagages, et un immense butin.

Ce ne fut qu'une année après cette victoire que l'Egypte fut rendue aux Turcs, par le traité d'Amiens, de 1802 ; tandis qu'ils l'auraient recouvrée, sans de nouvelles pertes, dès 1801, si le traité de Sidney-Smith eût été ratifié, comme il aurait dû l'être, puisqu'il n'avait fait que se conformer strictement aux instructions de son gouvernement.

Vous connaissez, messieurs, la brillante réception qui fut faite à Londres, à Sidney-Smith, lors de son retour dans sa patrie, en 1802 ; il y fut accueilli avec le plus grand enthousiasme; le surnom de *Dieu marin* lui fut décerné par le peuple. La ville de Rochester s'empressa de l'élire pour son représentant au Parlement, où il siégea dans les rangs de l'opposition, entre Shéridan et Fox.

J'appellerai votre attention sur un autre genre de services rendus à la nation Ottomane, par Sidney-Smith. Pendant son séjour à Constantinople, il avait acquis une grande influence sur Mahmoud-Kan II, qui, en 1808, succéda au sultan Mustapha IV, son frère. Sidney-Smith, par ses conseils, a puissamment contribué aux importantes révolutions politiques que Mahmoud-Kan II a introduites dans ses états, et notamment à la charte constitutionnelle que sous le titre de Hatti-Shériff de Gulaneh, cet immortel sultan a donnée au peuple Ottoman, charte dont le vice-roi d'Egypte, Méhémet-Ali, vient d'ordonner l'application, pour la révision de l'horrible procès intenté, dans la ville de Damas, par le fanatisme de secte, contre d'honorables Juifs, faussement accusés du meurtre d'un prêtre catholique.

Il est un plus grand service encore rendu a l'humanité, et auquel Sidney-Smith a eu la gloire de participer très-activement, c'est l'abolition de l'esclavage, dans toutes les colonies de la Grande-Bretagne. Grâce a l'ascendant irrésistible de l'opinion publique, les gouvernements de l'Europe seront forcés d'imiter ce sublime exemple, et de proscrire irrévocablement cet abominable trafic d'hommes, arrachés a leur patrie, pour être vendus, comme un vil bétail.

Je ne dois pas oublier que, dès l'année 1817, Sidney-Smith infatigable dans son dévouement a l'humanité, avait établi, à Londres et à Paris, une association anti-pirate, dont l'objet était de faire cesser la traite des blancs, exercée impunément, en présence de l'Europe civilisée, par les corsaires d'Alger, de Maroc et de Tunis.

Dans les dernières années d'une vie illustrée par tant d'actes mémorables, Sidney-Smith s'occupa de la recherche des moyens de sauvetage, pour les navires exposés aux tempêtes de la mer. Il a eu l'honneur d'être dans cette découverte l'un des inventeurs qui out le plus approché de la solution du problème de la garantie contre les naufrages.

Telle a été, messieurs, la carrière de Sidney-Smith, promu successivement à tous les grades de la marine, et jusqu'à celui d'Amiral de la Flotte Rouge d'Angleterre, que lui conféra le roi Guillaume IV ; il a été de plus décoré de tous les ordres des souverains de l'Europe, en reconnaissance des nombreux services qu'il leur a rendus.

A la vue du triste cercueil, qui contient les restes de Sidney-Smith, nous bornerons-nous au stérile récit de ses nobles actions ? Non, messieurs. Le vénérable évêque de l'église Anglicane, qui préside avec tant de dignité, à ces funérailles, vient d'invoquer, dans sa prière, le texte de l'Evangile, sur l'immortalité de l'âme, qu'il me soit permis d'ajouter à cette révélation du Christianisme, que les progrès de la science out démontré cette vérité, sans lui faire rien perdre du charme de l'espérance.

En effet, dans ce cercueil, que la tombe n'a point encore dérobé à nos regards, que reste-t-il ? Des débris d'organes inanimés. Mais ces nerfs, cette membrane qui les enveloppa, cette pulpe cérébrale qui les pénétra, qu'étaient-ils ? de la matière ! Ah ! de ces organes matériels, à la Sensation, il y a un abîme ! Et de la Sensation à la Pensée, un nouvel abîme ! Elle est donc immatérielle, cette Pensée, qui distingue si éminemment notre espèce, des autres êtres organisés !

N'est-ce pas la Pensée qui créa les arts et les sciences, qui, s'élevant jusqu'à la cause première, terme de ses conquêtes, y découvrit la Divinité, dont elle établit le culte universel, comme le plus puissant mobile de la civilisation ?

Combien n'est-il pas consolant, au milieu des parens et des nombreux amis qui entourent cette tombe, d'y professer, d'y confirmer le dogme de l'immortalité de l'âme, et de pouvoir y proclamer que Sidney-Smith n'est pas mort tout entier ?

Oui, messieurs, le principe intellectuel qui nous anime, est incontestablement un être, et cet être est immortel. Pourrait-il donc s'anéantir, quand les organes matériels de nos corps sont eux-mêmes éternels dans leurs éléments ?

L'orateur qui vient de retracer avec tant de talent, la carrière de l'illustre Amiral, vous a signalé la restitution des cendres de l'empereur Napoleon a la France, par le gouvernement Britannique, comme un gage de la parfaite harmonie, heureusement rétablie entre les deux nations. Je partage ce favorable augure, et tel fut le vœu le plus intime de Sidney-Smith, qui ne cessa de répéter que la civilisation du monde tenait essentiellement à l'alliance de la France et de l'Angleterre.

A l'aspect des restes de Napoléon, traversant l'Océan pour recouvrer un tombeau dans sa patrie, j'aime à prévoir que les restes de Sidney-Smith seront pareillement réclamés par son gouvernement, et qu'à leur tour, ils traverseront la mer, pour être déposés à Westminster, dans le lieu consacré à la sépulture des rois et des reines, ainsi qu'à celle des grands hommes de l'Angleterre.

SKETCH OF THE HISTORY AND POSSESSIONS OF THE ORDER IN IRELAND.

The Order of Knights Templars was introduced into Ireland about the year 1174, by Richard, surnamed Strongbow, Earl of Pembroke, or Strigul. A Priory was founded by him in that year, under the invocation of St. John the Baptist, at Kilmainham, in the County of Dublin, for Knights Templars, (see Archdall's Monasticon Hibernicum, pages 222 et seq.) and King Henry II. granted his confirmation. Hugh de Cloghall was the first Prior, and enjoyed that office till about the year 1190. The noble founder had enfeoffed the Prior in the whole lands of Kilmainham; and dying in 1176, was interred in Christ Church. The two Orders of Knights Templars and Hospitallers were confirmed the same year. After this, Hugh Tirrel bestowed upon the Prior of this hospital the lands of Chapel-Izod and Kilmehanock, "free from all secular services and burthens, with all liberties and free customs, in wood and open country, in meadows and pastures, in roads and paths," &c. &c.

Kilmainham continued to be the Grand Priory or Preceptory of the Templars, till their suppression in 1312; and the Superior of the Order, according to Sir James Ware, sat in the House of Peers as a Baron, a privilege enjoyed, as regarded the military orders, only by the Grand Priors of Kilmainham for the Templars, and of Wexford for the Hospitallers. He is styled by Archdall, quoting different ancient records, sometimes *Prior*, and sometimes *Master*, as in the case of Maurice de Prendergast, 1205 and 1210; sometimes *Preceptor*, as "D. Walens, Preceptor of the Templars, 1247;" sometimes *Grand Master*, as "1266, Robert was Grand Master of the Templars in Ireland this year." In 1288, we find "William Fitz-Roger was *Prior* this year, and Thomas de Thoulouse *Master* of the Templars;" in 1296, "Walter le Bachelour was *Master*, and William de Rosse was *Prior*, who the same year was made Lord Deputy of Ireland." He continued in these offices till 1302, when he was made Chief Justice; and appears in this year also to have preferred his complaint against the sheriff of Dublin for an illegal seizure, as "the *Master* of the Templars." And in 1309, Gerald, son of Maurice, Lord of Kerry, is spoken of as "the last *Grand Prior* of the Order."

The subordinate governors of the Order appear to have been styled indiscriminately Preceptors or Commanders; and their castles or estates Preceptories or Commanderies. These were (according to Ware and Archdall) at Clontarf, in the county of Dublin, founded in Henry II.'s reign, as it is supposed by the Nettervilles; St. Sepulchre, in the city of Dublin or its suburbs, near the place where the Archbishop's palace stands; Kilsaran, in the county of Louth, founded in the 12th century by Maud de Lacie; Kilbarry and Killure, the one about a mile and a half from Waterford, and the other two miles east of that city, in the county of the same name, both founded in the 12th century, the founders unknown; Crooke, in the harbour of Waterford, four miles east of the city, founded in the 13th century, by the Baron of Curragmore; Clonaul, in Tipperary, as also one at Thurles, in the same county, where a castle now standing was, according to the tradition of the country, for no record exists, the castle of the Knights Templars; Teach-Temple, or Temple House, in the county of Sligo, founded in the time of Henry III.; Mourne, in the county of Cork, founded in the reign of King John, by Alexander de Sancta Helena; Killergy, or Killarge, in the county of Carlow, "founded in the reign of King John, by Gilbert de Borard, for Knights Templars, under the invocation of St. John the Baptist; Kilclogan, in the county of Wexford, founded in the 13th century by the family of O'More, which appears to have had a large estate attached to it, from the report made in the thirty-second year of King Henry VIII., quoted by Archdall, page 748; and Dundrum, in the county of Down, where is a strong castle, now in ruins, said to have been built by Sir John de Courcy."

All these Commanderies and Preceptories were, together with the Grand Priory of Kilmainham, granted on the abolition of the Order, to the Knights of St. John of Jerusalem, in whose possession they continued till the dissolution of monasteries in the reign of King Henry VIII.

It may not be uninteresting to add the account of Archdall regarding the circumstances which attended the persecution and attempted destruction of the Order *in Ireland*.

"In 1307, Walter de Ewias, or de Aqua, being Prior, the King (Edward II.) transmitted to John Wogan, Justiciary of Ireland, the order made for the suppression of the Knights Templars in England, on the Wednesday after the feast of the Epiphany, enjoining him to have it executed in Ireland without delay, and before the rumour of what was done in England could reach this kingdom. The mandate was accordingly obeyed, and on the morrow of the Purification the Templars were everywhere seized."

"1309. The King, by writ, dated September the 29th, did further command the said Justiciary to apprehend, without delay, all the Templars that had not yet been seized, and them safely to keep in the Castle of Dublin, together with those who had been before apprehended."

"1311. On the petition of Henry Danet, or De Tanet, the late Master of the Templars, and the other members of that Order, the King, by writ, dated December 4th, did grant for their support the manors of Kilclogan, Crooke, and Kilbarry."

"1312. This year, on the morrow of St. Lucia the Virgin, the moon appeared variously coloured, on which day it was finally determined that the Order of Knights Templars should be totally abolished."

"The trial of the Templars was conducted with great solemnity in the city of Dublin, before Friar Richard Balybyn, minister of the Order of the Dominicans in Ireland, Friar Philip de Slane, lecturer of the same, and Friar Hugh St. Leger. Amongst other witnesses against the Knights, were Roger de Heton, Guardian of the Franciscan Friars; Walter de Prendergast, their lecturer; Thomas, the Abbot; Simon, the Prior of the Abbey of St. Thomas-the-Martyr, and Roger, Prior of the Augustinian Friary in Dublin. The depositions against the Templars were weakly supported, yet they were condemned; but more indeed through blind compliance with the prevailing practice throughout other parts of Europe, than any demerits being proved against their persons. Their lands and possessions of every kind were bestowed upon the Knights of St. John of Jerusalem by the Pope, which grant was confirmed by the King, who at the same time entered a protest of his rights against the assumed power of the Pope."

EXTRACT OF CHARTER BY KING JAMES THE IV. OF SCOTLAND, CONFIRMING GRANTS BY KINGS MALCOLM IV., ALEXANDER II., ALEXANDER III., JAMES II., AND JAMES III., TO THE KNIGHTS OF THE HOSPITAL AND TEMPLE.

Jacobus Dei Gracia Rex Scotorum. Omnibus probis hominibus tocius terre sue clericis et laicis salutem. Sciatis nos quasdam cartas et euidentias per quondam nostros illustrissimos predecessores Scotorum reges factas et concessas Deo et Sancto Hospitali de Jerusalem et Fratribus Eiusdem Militie Templi Salomonis, videlicet, CARTAM confirmacionis quondam serenissimi patris nostri cuius anime propicietur. Deus factam super carta confirmacionis quondam aui nostri Jacobi Secundi regis Scotorum in qua inseruntur quatuor carte quondam predecessorum nostrorum Malcolmi et Alexandri Scotorum regum facte dicto Hospitali de Jerusalem, nunc Torfiching nuncupat. ac ffratribus eiusdem de nonnullis elemosinis terris toftis libertatibus tholoneis consuetudinibus in empcionibus et vendicionibus qualitercunque contingen. amerciamentis et priuilegiis ac super feodo et forisfactura suorum libere tenencium ut in dictis quatuor cartis predecessorum nostrorum in eisdem cartis confirmacionis in forma maiori insertis plenius constat et continetur de mandato, nostro uisam lectam inspectam diligenter examinatam, sanam integram non rasem non cancellatam nec in aliqua sua parte suspectam ad plenum intellexisse sub hac forma:—**(1.)** Jacobus Dei gracia rex Scotorum, omnibus probis hominibus tocius terre sue clericis et laicis salutem,—Sciatis nos quasdam cartas et euidentias per nostras illustrissimos, predecessores factas et concessas, Deo et sancto Hospitali de Jerusalem ffratribus eiusdem militie Templi Salomonis, videlicet, Cartam confirmacionis quondam nostri serenissimi progenitoris Jacobi Secundi Scotorum regis factam super cartis quondam Malcolmi et Alexandri Scotorum regum dicto Hospitali de Jerusalem, nunc Torfiching nuncupato ac ffratribus eiusdem de nonnullis elemosinis terris toftis libertatibus tholoneis consuetudinibus in empcionibus et vendicionibus et qualitercunque contingen. amerciamentis et priuilegiis vt in quatuor cartis predecessorum nostrorum in dicta carta confirmacionis in maiori forma insertis continetur de mandato, nostro uisam lectam inspectam et diligenter examinatam sanam integram non rasam non cancellatam nec in aliqua sui parte suspectam, ad plenum intellexisse, sub hac forma. **(2.)** Jacobus Dei gracia rex Scotorum, Omnibus probis hominibus tocius terre nostre clericis et laicis salutem, Sciatis nos uidisse inspexisse et diligenter examinasse cartas et euidentias illustrissimorum progenitorum et antecessorum nostrorum, viz. Malcolmi Alexandri et Alexandri regum Scocie, quarum tenores de uerbo in verbum sequuntur. [Here follow the respective grants of confirmation by the above Sovereigns, three of which are addressed to the Hospitallers, and one (by Alexander II.) to the Knights Templars. These we could have wished to have quoted at large, but find it would exceed our limits. The Charter then proceeds] —"Quasquidam" cartas et euidencias tam dictas cartas confirmacionum quondam patris et aui nostrorum qua measdam quatuor cartas predictorum predecessorum ac donaciones concessiones libertates priuilegia ceteraque omnia et singula in eisdem contentis in omnibus suis punctis et articulis condicionibus et modis ac circumstanciis suis quibuscunque forma pariter et effectu in omnibus et per omnia ut premissum est approbamus ratificamus et pro nobis et successoribus nostris pro perpetuo confirmamus. Ac insuper, ubi in dictis cartis non clare constat in illo termino 'de tholoneis' nos tamen ob singulares specialesque fauorem, amorem, et delectionem, quos gerimus ergo dilectum familiarem militem, nostrumque consiliarium delectum Wilelmum Knollis, modernum preceptorem eiusdem Loci de Torfichin, nostrum thesaurarium, Volumus, Concessimus, et hac presenti carta nostra Concedimus eidem Preceptori et suis successoribus Preceptoribus de Torfiching ut sint liberi a solucione alicuius custume de quibuscunque bonis et mercanciis suis destinandis per eosdem ad partes extra-marinas pro solucione ipsius Preceptoris responsionis, que vero responsio extendit ad ducentos ducatos, et quod annuatim in nostro saccario videatur ad quantam summam custume dicta bona se extendunt et tantum eidem Preceptori allocatur. In cuius rei testimonium, huic presenti carte nostre confirmacionis magnum sigillum apponi precipimus. Testibus, &c. Apud Edinburge decimo nono die mensis Octobris anno domini millesimo quadringentesimo octuajesimo octauo et regni nostri primo.

PROCLAMATION BY THE FREEMASONS OF EUROPE,

—DATED AT COLOGNE ON THE RHINE
1535,

S. M. G. D. O.

We, the Elect Masters of the Venerable Society sacred to John, or of the Social Order of Freemasons, Rulers of the Lodges or Tabernacles, constituted at London, Edinburgh, Vienna, Amsterdam, Paris, Lyons, Frankfort, Hamburgh, Antwerp, Rotterdam, Madrid, Venice, Ghent, Regiomonte, Brussels, Dantzic, Middleburgh,

and in the City of Cologne, in Chapter assembled in the said City of Cologne, in the year, month, and days aftermentioned. Our Preses being the Master of the Lodge established in this City,—a venerable Brother and most learned, prudent, and judicious man, called to preside over these deliberations, by our unanimous vote;—do, by these letters addressed to all the above-mentioned Lodges,—to our Brethren present and future, declare, that forasmuch as we have been considering the designs, which in these calamitous times embroiled, by Civil dissensions and discord, have been imputed to our foresaid Society, and to all the Brethren belonging to this Order of Freemasons, or of John, opinions, machinations, secret, as well as openly detected; all which are utterly foreign to us, and to the Spirit, Design, and Precepts, of the Association. It moreover appears that we, the Members of this Order, (chiefly because we are bound by those inscrutable secrets of our connection and covenant which are most sacredly kept by us all,) in order that we may be more effectually vilified among the uninitiated and profane, and that we may be devoted to public execration, are accused of the crime of reviving the Order of the Templars, and commonly designated by that appellation, as if we had combined and conspired for the purpose of recovering, as Members of that Order, its property and possessions, and avenging the death of the last Grand Master, who presided over that Order, on the posterity of the Kings and Princes who were guilty of the crime, and who were the authors of the extinction of said Order; as if, with that view, we were exciting schisms in the Churches, and disturbance and sedition in the Temporal Government and Dominions; as if we were influenced by hatred and enmity against the Pope, the Chief Pontiff, the Emperor, and all Kings; as if obeying no external power, but only the superiors and elected of our own Association, which is spread throughout the whole World,—we executed their secret mandates and clandestine designs, by the private intercourse of correspondence and emissaries; as if, in fine, we admitted none into our Mysteries but those who, after being scrutinised and tried by bodily tortures, became bound and devoted to our Conclaves. Therefore, having all these considerations in view, it hath seemed to us expedient, and even absolutely necessary, to expound the true state and origin of our Order, and to what it tends, as an institute of charity itself, according as these principles are recognised and approved by those who are most versant in the Highest Craft, and by masters enlightened in the genuine sciences of the Institution, and to give forth to the Lodges or Conclaves of our society the principles thus expounded, digested, and organised, as an examplar authenticated by our signatures, whereby a perpetual record may remain of this our renewed covenant, and the unshaken integrity of our purpose; and also in case, through the daily increasing propensity of the people to animosities, enmity, intolerance, and wars, this our society should hereafter be more and more oppressed, inasmuch as to be unable to maintain its standing and consolidation, and thus be dispersed to some distant regions of the earth; and in case, through lapse of time, the society itself should become less observant of its integrity, purity, and incorruptibility, nevertheless, in better times and more convenient circumstances, there may remain, if not the whole, yet perhaps one or other of the duplicates of these presents, by which standard the Order, if subverted, may be restored, and if corrupted or estranged from its purpose and designs, may be reformed. For THESE CAUSES, by these our universal letters, compiled according to the context of the most ancient monuments which are extant, concerning the objects of the institution,—the rites and customs of our most ancient and most secret order,—We, Elect Masters, influenced by the love of the true light, do, by the most solemn sanctions, adjure all fellow-labourers, to whom these presents now or in time hereafter may come, that they withdraw not themselves from the truth contained in this document. Moreover, to the enlightened, as well as to the darker world, whose common safety concerns and strongly interests us, we announce and proclaim,—

(A) That the Society of Free Masons, or Order of Brethren attached to the solemnities of St. John, derive not their origin from the Knights Templars, nor from any other order of knights, ecclesiastic or secular, detached or connected with one or more, neither have any or the least communication with them, directly, or through any manner of intermediate tie; that they are more ancient than any order of knights of this description, and existed in Palestine and Greece, as well as in every part of the Roman Empire, long before the Holy Wars, and the times of the expeditions of the above mentioned knights into Palestine.

That from various monuments of approved authenticity, the fact is to us quite notorious, that this our Association took its origin from the time when first on account of the various Sects of the Christian World, a few adepts distinguished by their life, their moral doctrine, and their sacred interpretation of the Arcanic Truths, withdrew themselves from the multitude; for the learned and enlightened men, who lived in those times, (the true Christians who were least infected with the errors of Paganism,) when they considered, that through a corrupt religion, schisms, and not peace, and neither toleration nor charity, but atrocious wars, were promulgated, bound themselves by a most solemn Oath, in order more effectually to preserve uncontaminated the Moral Principles of this Religion, which are implanted in the mind of man, that to these they would devote themselves; that the True Light, arising gradually out of darkness, might proceed to the subduing of superstitions, by the cultivation of every Human virtue, and to the establishment of peace and comfort among men. That under these benign auspices the Masters of this community are called Brethren dedicated to John, following the example and invitation of John the Baptist, Precursor of the Rising Light,—first among the Martyr Stars of the Morning.

That these Doctors and Scribes who were also, according to the custom of those times, called Masters, did, from the most experienced and best of the Disciples, collect and choose fellow labourers, whence arose the name of Socius. When others were elected, but not chosen, they were designed, after the manner of the Hebrew, Greek, and Roman Philosophers, by the appellation of Disciple.

(B) That our Association now, as formerly, consists of the Three Degrees of Disciple, Fellow, and

Master. The last, or Masters, admitting of Elect Masters and Superior Elect Masters. But that all Associations or Fraternities so called, who admit of more or other denominations or subdivisions, and who ascribe to themselves another origin, and, intermeddling with Political and Ecclesiastical affairs, make promises and protestations under whatever titles they may assume, of Freemasons and Brethren, attached to the solemnities of John, or others which belong not to our Order, are to be expelled and ejected from it as Schismatics.

(Γ) That among the Doctors, Masters of this Order, cultivating the Sciences of Mathematics, Astronomy, and other Studies, a mutual interchange of doctrine and light was maintained, which led to the practice of electing out of those who were already Elect Masters, one in particular, who, as excelling the rest, should be venerated as Supreme Elect Master or Patriarch. Being known only to the Elect Master, he was regarded both as the Visible and Invisible Head and Chief of our whole Association; so that, according to this Ordnance, the Supreme Master and Patriarch, though known to very few, yet still exists. The premises being compiled from the mass of parchments and charter of the Order itself, committed, by authority of our Patrons, with the sacred documents, in future to the charge of our Preses and his successors; and being herewith diligently compared by W. E. Santona, by authority of the same illustrious Patriarch, ordain and command as follows:

(Δ) The government of our society, the mode and

rule according to which the flaming light may be imparted and diffused among the illuminated brethren, as well as the profane world, rest entirely with the highest Elect Masters. To them belongs the charge of watching and taking care, lest the members, of whatever rank or order, should attempt any thing contrary to the true principles of our Society. Upon the same chiefs of the Society are incumbent the defence of the Order, the preservation and safeguard of its welfare, which, should occasion require, they are to protect at the expense of their fortunes, and the risk of their lives, against all who attack our Institution, whatsoever and wheresoever this may be done.

(E) To us it is by no means clear, that this association of brethren, prior to the year one thousand four hundred and forty, were known by any other denomination than that of *Joannite Brethren*; but at that time we are informed, the fraternity, especially in Valence in Flanders, began to be called by the name of *Free Masons*, from which period, in some parts of Hanover, Hospitals began to be built by the aid and pecuniary assistance of the Brethren, for those who laboured under the Sacred Fire, called St. Anthony's Evil.

(Z) Although in works of benevolence we pay no regard to religion or country, we however consider it safe and necessary hitherto to receive none into our Order but those who, in the society of the profane and unenlightened, are professedly Christians. In conducting the inquisition and trial of those who apply for the initiation of the First Degree, which is that of Disciple, no bodily tortures are employed, but only those trials which tend to develope the nature, inclinations, and dispositions of the Candidates.

(H) To those duties which are commanded and undertaken by a solemn oath, are added those of fidelity and obedience to the secular rulers, lawfully placed over us.

(Θ) The principle on which we act, and all these our efforts, to whatever purpose and direction they may tend, are expressed in these two precepts: —"Love and regard all men as Brethren and Relations —render to God what is God's, and to Cæsar what is Cæsar's."

(I) The Secrets and Mysteries which veil our undertakings conduce to this end,—that without ostentation we may do good, and without disunion of action, prosecute our designs to the uttermost.

(K) We celebrate annually the Memory of St. John the Forerunner of Christ, and Patron of our Community.

(Λ) These, and the rest of the corresponding ceremonies of the Institution, though conducted in the meetings of the Brethren by signs, or speech, or otherwise, do nevertheless differ totally from the rites of the Churches.

(M) The above is considered a Brother of the Joannite Society, or a Freemason, who, in a lawful manner, by the help, and under the direction of some Elect Master, with the assistance of at least seven Brethren, is initiated into our mysteries, and who is ready to prove his adoption by the Signs and Tokens which are used by other Brethren; but in which Signs and Words are included, those which are in use in The Edinburgh Lodge or Tabernacle and its Affiliated Lodges; as also in the Hamburgh, Rotterdam, and Middleburg Tabernacles, and in that which is found erected at Venice, whose ministrations and labours, though they be ordained after the manner of the Scots, differ not from those which are used by us, in so far as they respect the origin, design, and institution.

(N) This our Society, being superintended by one General Prince, while the different governments of which it consists are ruled by various Superior Masters, adapted to various regions and kingdoms, as need requires. Nothing is more necessary than a certain conformity among all those who are dispersed throughout the whole World, as members of one aggregate body; and likewise an intercourse of missionaries and correspondence harmonising with them, and with their doctrines in all places.—Wherefore, these present letters, testifying the nature and spirit of our Society, shall be sent to all and sundry Colleges of the Order as yet existing. For these reasons abovementioned, nineteen uniform duplicates of letters, composed in this form, exactly of the same tenor, confirmed and corroborated by our subscriptions and signatures, are given at Cologne on the Rhine, in the year one thousand five hundred and thirty-five, on the twenty-fourth day of the month of June, according to the Era, designated Christian.

Harmanius + Carlton, Jo. Bruce, Fr. V. Upna, Cornelius Banning, De Colligni, Virieux, Johani Schröder, Kofman, 1535, Jacobus Praepositus, A. Nobel, Ignatius de la Terre, Dona Jacob Uttenhove, Falk Nacolus, Va Noot, Phillippus Melanthon, Hugssen, Wormer Abel.

Certified in form to the printed examplar, deposited into the Archives of the Gr. and Sublime Chap. of the Temples Interior, Sitting in the East of Namur.

The Gr. Chancellor of that Chief Chap.
De Marchot.

LIST OF CHEVALIERS,

List of Chevaliers,

Whose Armorial Bearings are emblazoned upon the *Gothic Gateway* at the beginning of this Work, and to whom the Plate is affectionately dedicated by their Friend and Brother,

James Burnes.

Sir William Sidney Smith, G.C.B.
&c. &c. &c. &c.
Late Regent and Prince Magistral of the
Order of the Temple.

Outram.	Hair.	Gibson.	Erskine.	Burnes.	Le Geyt.
Le Messurier.	Kennedy.			Bogle.	Holmes.
Chalmers.	Campbell.			Campbell.	Lushington.
Macan.	Shaw.	ARMS		Fitzgerald.	Bortoleme.
		OF			
		THE ORDER.			
Dunlop.	Le Geyt.			Pearson.	Simson.
Laurie.	Winchester.			Ramsay.	Pringle.

James Burnes,
Knight of Aquitaine, and of the Royal Guelphic Order,
Grand Prior of India

Bailiff of Berne.   Harris.

Whose Armorial Bearings are emblazoned upon the *Gothic Gateway* at the beginning of this Work, and to whom the Plate is affectionately dedicated by their Friend and Brother,

James Burnes.

Sɪʀ Wɪʟʟɪᴀᴍ Sɪᴅɴᴇʏ Sᴍɪᴛʜ, G.C.B.
&c.   &c.   &c.   &c.
Late Regent and Prince Magistral of the
Order of the Temple.

ARMS
of
THE ORDER.

- Outram.
- Hair.
- Gibson.
- Erskine.
- Burnes.
- Le Geyt.
- Le Messurier.
- Kennedy.
- Bogle.
- Holmes.
- Chalmers.
- Campbell.
- Campbell.
- Lushington.
- Macan.
- Shaw.
- Fitzgerald.
- Bortoleme.
- Dunlop.
- Le Geyt.
- Pearson.
- Simson.

- Laurie.
- Winchester.
- Ramsay.
- Pringle.

JAMES BURNES,
Knight of Aquitaine, and of the Royal Guelphic
Order,
Grand Prior of India.

- Bailiff of Berne.
- Harris.

Copyright © 2021 by Alicia Editions
Credits images: Canva
All rights reserved.
No part of this book may be reproduced in any form or by any electronic or mechanical means, including information storage and retrieval systems, without written permission from the author, except for the use of brief quotations in a book review.

www.ingramcontent.com/pod-product-compliance
Lightning Source LLC
LaVergne TN
LVHW091711190726
843493LV00001B/257